102 WAYS

TO SAVE MONEY

FOR AND AT

WALT DISNEY WORLD

BY LOU MONGELLO

COPYRIGHTS, TRADEMARKS, ETC.

This book is unauthorized and unofficial. It has not been reviewed by The Walt Disney Company and is in no way authorized, endorsed or approved by the company, it's sponsors, partners or affiliates. I simply wish to share my love of Walt Disney World with readers, in an effort to enhance their enjoyment and appreciation the Walt Disney World® Resort.

My Guarantee

This book has been assembled by pulling together years' worth of experiences in the Disney parks. Your goal should not be to use all 102 strategies in the same vacation — it's not logistically feasible; however, if you select the strategies that are best for your family and your unique situation, I guarantee you will improve the value of your vacation experience for your hard-earned dollar — **without** sacrificing any of the magic of the Disney vacation.

And I guarantee that if you use even just a few of the tips in this book, that you will be able to save money for and during your next Walt Disney World vacation. If you don't, let me know what you did and why it didn't work, and I'll gladly refund the purchase price of your book.

I encourage you to share your experiences with me and the WDW Radio community by visiting our Facebook page at http://Facebook.com/WDWRadio, or with me directly via Twitter — I'm http://Twitter.com/LouMongello or follow me on Facebook at http://Facebook.com/LouMongello. You can also email me directly at Lou@WDWRadio.com and share your experiences!

Thank you once again, and I sincerely hope you have a truly magical, memorable time on your next Walt Disney World vacation!

— Lou Mongello

CONTENTS

8 Introduction

18 The Basics

22 Before You Go

34 When To Go

48 How To Go

66 Tickets

86 Disney Resorts

102 To Book A Package... or Not

108 Dining

126 What To Pack... Or Ship

134 While You're There

156 Shopping

172 Bonus!

194 Resources and Links

102
WAYS
TO SAVE MONEY
FOR AND AT
WALT DISNEY WORLD

BY LOU MONGELLO

INTRODUCTION

Walt Disney World has been a part of my life for as long as I can remember. Growing up, trips to Walt's newest vacation destination were a cherished part of my family experiences. My first visit was in November of 1971, just weeks after the park opened its gates for the very first time. My father loved Disney and what it represented, and he wanted to be there as quickly as he could (the apple doesn't fall far from the tree, obviously). That first visit led to our annual pilgrimages to what would quickly become our "favorite family fun park."

And much like the Griswolds, we would load up the "family truckster" and make the drive from New Jersey to Florida. Even if Walt Disney World wasn't our only destination (much to my dismay), we visited the parks at least once a year. I realized much later in life that we went to Walt Disney World not because of the attractions and shows, but because of the memories we were creating on each visit. They were the days before cell phones, handheld video games, and many of life's other distractions. The journey was as much fun as the destination, as we played "The Cereal Game," "The License Plate Game," and other ridiculous time-wasters that (unbeknownst to me), were bringing us closer as a family.

When we visited Walt Disney World, I can fondly remember checking in to the Contemporary, always agape at the sight of the cavernous Grand Canyon Concourse, and fascinated that a monorail was whooshing by overhead. The sounds of the manual doors on the monorail cars would quickly become a comfortable sound, that let me know that my family and I were in our "second home." I think I spent as many hours in the Fiesta Fun Center as I did in the Magic Kingdom, but it was really the time spent with family that solidified these lasting memories.

Over the years, I would continue to visit Walt Disney World not just with my family, but with friends, as I found myself wanting to share my love of this place that meant so much to me with others as well.

While studying at Villanova University, my Spring Break trips weren't spent in Cabo San Lucas... but in the Magic Kingdom. After graduating from Seton Hall University School of Law, I celebrated with (of course), a vacation to Disney.

I served as law clerk to the Presiding Judge of the largest vicinage in the the State of New Jersey, and practiced law actively for nine years. In 1995, I formed Imagine Enterprises, a computer consulting and web development firm, and was formerly the Chief Technology Officer for a multimodality medical imaging company in Edison, New Jersey. But during this entire time, my love and passion for Disney never waned. And with each visit, I continued to try and learn all I could about this truly magical place that drew me (and millions of others) back year after year.

In 2003, as a personal challenge, I set out to write a book — To see if I could do it, and to have it validated by being published. I learned everything I could about the book publishing industry, and eventually signed a multi-book deal with the Intrepid Traveler publishing company (thank you, Sally and Kelly!). I wrote the book I wanted to read, which was a Walt Disney World Trivia Book (*available on Amazon.com* — http://www.WDWRadio.com/Amazonbooks) (I had all this "useless knowledge" of Disney minutiae rolling around in my head, so it made perfect sense). So, the idea for the book was formulated out of my personal interest in some of the lesser-known facts about the parks, general Walt Disney World trivia, and the "magic" that drives tens of millions adults and children on recurring pilgrimages to the resort.

I created a small, two-page web site promoting the book, which eventually turned into articles (it's what we called blog posts back in 2004), discussion forums, a second Walt Disney World Trivia Book (*available on Amazon.com*) and much more than I had even anticipated.

I started podcasting in early 2005, realizing that this very new technology would allow me to share my passion for Disney in a new, much more powerful way. I didn't know if anyone would even find the show, let alone listen to me talk about Disney each week for an hour or so, but thanks to a growing group of incredible members of my WDW Radio "family," the show has been awarded Best Travel Podcast for 2006, 2007, 2008, 2009, 2010, 2011, 2012 and 2013. I continued to grow my offerings to include a continuing series of Audio Guides to Walt Disney World CDs, as well as videos and live broadcasts for http://WDWRadio.com.

But the most important part of everything I've ever done has been the creation of our Dream Team Project to help grant the wishes of children with serious illnesses to visit Walt Disney World through the Make-A-Wish Foundation of America. To date, we have raised more than $250,000.00. To learn more about the personal reasons why I started the Project, or to find out how you can help be a part of it, please visit http://DreamTeamProject.org. (Dad, this is for you.)

So my little book idea somehow evolved into a business, and in 2008 I took a huge leap of faith. I left my "real-life" day job behind, sold the house I thought I would live in forever, packed up the minivan and drove to Florida — for good. I wanted to pursue my passion, and follow a dream of sharing my love for Walt Disney World with others. In addition to the site, show, videos, and live broadcasts, I also host events, have become a regular commentator on Fox 35 News in Orlando, and speak to groups, businesses, conferences and schools about the magic of Disney and the power of social and new media. *(You can learn more about me or book me to speak by visiting my web site at http://LouMongello.com)*

And throughout my 40+ years of visiting Walt Disney World, I've continued to strive to learn all I can not just about the parks, their history, stories and details, but also about gaining practical experience and advice in order to have a more enjoyable, experiential, and memorable vacation. And with that comes getting the most value for your vacation dollar so you can do and enjoy more, while spending less.

I am writing this because I know how hard families work to save the money for a Disney vacation. I saw how hard my parents strived to give my brother and me the most magical experience, and as a parent myself, I now do the same for my children and family.

Today, Walt Disney World is a significantly bigger, in some ways more daunting, and certainly more expensive vacation experience for a family to plan for than it was for my parents. *(Remember when it cost under $5.00 to go to the Magic Kingdom? The A through E ticket books!?)* But the memories of my vacations are so precious to me, I want to be sure as many people as possible are able to give their children what my parents gave to me, and what I am striving to do for my own family.

By purchasing and reading this book, you will learn how to maximize your vacation dollar without sacrificing the quality of vacation experience that Walt Disney World has to offer. In fact, I think you will have a much richer, memorable time because of all the new things you will be able to see, experience (and yes, even eat!) You will discover that there are many ways you can plan to save before, during, and even AFTER your Disney vacation. Look for the blue highlighted sections throughout the book to see just how much you can save! It's not difficult to save — it's just a matter of doing your homework and putting together a plan that works for you and your family. And I'm here to help!

In addition to this book, you can find many other valuable Walt Disney World vacation planning resources at WDWRadio.com, including the podcast, blog, videos, live broadcasts, special events, discussion forums, my Walt Disney World Trivia Books and my virtual audio walking tours of the parks.

Why 102?

Why call this book 102 ways to save, rather than the more common 101? Well, in Disney theme park language, if an attraction is internally referred to as "101," it means the attraction is closed and/or not properly functioning. When an attraction is back up and running, and making its usual magic for guests, it is referred to as "102."

I see this book as your first step toward making sure your Disney vacation becomes a financial reality, and that you and your family are "up and running" into a magical adventure that will build cherished memories for years to come.

And when you visit the parks, whether with your family, friends, or solo, remember that sometimes you will never know the true value of a moment until it becomes a memory, so savor every minute!

Just so you know...

Accuracy and Other Impossible Dreams...

All facts and statistics are accurate as of the time this book goes to press. But... (here's where the "recovering attorney" in me comes out), Walt Disney World is constantly changing. So, what that means is that while I tried to ensure the accuracy of the information at press time, things may have (literally) changed overnight, so please be sure you double check and verify pricing, availability and offers when making your plans.

Do you want to help contribute or add something to the 102 Ways guide? Do you have any questions, comments, or suggestions — or notice that I may have missed something? You can let me know by emailing me personally at lou@wdwradio.com.

Dedication

This book would not have been possible without the love and support of my family and friends. My wife, Deanna has always been my best friend, partner, teammate and loving supporter of everything I've done. I wouldn't be where I am today without her. She makes me a better man, and because of her my dreams have come true. My daughter, Marion, and my son, Nicolas are the two greatest joys in my life. They have forever changed me as a person, and I'm so fortunate to be able to share Disney with them and see it through their eyes. You were worth waiting for. To my mom, who has always been my biggest champion, my love of Disney came from you and the times we spent together. Thank you for your wisdom, lessons, patience and guidance. For my brother, with whom I've shared more laughs than I can remember, and who has always been there for me. And my dad... I miss you incredibly and hope that I have made you proud. I'm here because of you. I feel your guiding hand on my shoulder, and so much of what I do is in your name and honor.

Acknowledgment

There are far too many people with whom I have crossed paths that have had a profound impact on my life and its many changing directions to thank here. I believe that every person who enters your life is for a reason and a purpose. You may not have realized it at the time, but each of you has touched my life, and for that I am forever grateful. And many of those people have helped me along the way as well…

To Christy Viszoki, who has been an incredible supporter, contributor, help and friend. Words can't describe my gratitude. If there were more people like you in the world, it would be a much better place. The best is yet to come!!

To the so many people who have encouraged and assisted in ways they may not even have known *(and please forgive me, as I know I'm forgetting SO many of you):* Glenn Whelan, Scott Otis, Beci Mahnken, Valerie Drew, Tony Caggiano, Jim Korkis, Ryan Wilson, John Capos, Tim Foster, Larsen and Stephanie Eisenberg, ALL of The Box People (you know who you are—I love you all!!), the WDW Radio blog writers, Tim Street, Henry Work, Todd Andrlik, Jenn Selke, the members of the WDW Radio Running Team (Go Blue!!) and Dream Team Project, Beatrice Feeney, my friends at DDG: Brian Blackmore, Alex Maher, Ron Cohee, Casey Jones, and Mark Seppala, Jeff and Sarah Li, J., Chuck L., Mike, Jeremy, Marc, Zanna, Christine Z., Sally and Kelly, my entire WDW Radio family… there are SO many more of you who have inspired, helped, motivated, driven, laughed with, listened to, shared with and taught me—I cannot thank you enough for this "E-Ticket" ride in life which I am so blessed to be on. I hope this journey together never ends…

To the Cast Members and friends at The Walt Disney Company, thank you for being the dreamers and doers and keeping Walt Disney's legacy and dreams alive and in action every day.

And to you, the reader, thank you for letting me be a small part of your Walt Disney World vacation and experience. I am blessed and thankful for the ability to share my love of Disney with you in this and so many other ways.

And I am most grateful to God, who has put me on this path and given me His love, blessings and guidance, and who has taught me to think less, trust more, and have faith.

Thank you...

102
WAYS
TO SAVE MONEY
FOR AND AT

WALT DISNEY WORLD

BY LOU MONGELLO

THE BASICS

What IS Walt Disney World and WHY Do I Need to Prepare for my Visit?

One of the most important parts of a Walt Disney World® Resort vacation is what takes places even before you leave the house. Planning is the key to making the most of your vacation — and to get the most wonderful experience possible for your vacation dollar. Let's face it: a vacation to Walt Disney World is unlike almost any travel destination. Consider some numbers:

Walt Disney World® Resort property encompasses 47 square miles; it is as large as the city of San Francisco!

Within the 47 square miles (double the size of Manhattan!), there are countless experiences that await you, all found within:

- 4 theme parks: (Magic Kingdom® Park, Epcot®, Disney's Hollywood Studios®, and Disney's Animal Kingdom® Theme Park)

- 2 water parks: Blizzard Beach and Typhoon Lagoon

- 23 resort hotels that offer legendary Disney service

- 4 18-hole golf courses (Osprey Ridge, Palm, Magnolia, Lake Buena Vista) and 1 9-hole walking course (Oak Trail)

- 2 miniature golf courses (Winter Summerland and Fantasia Gardens), each of which has 2 18-hole courses of play.

- Water sports and activities such as boating, parasailing, fishing and more

- 2 dinner shows (Hoop Dee Doo Revue and the Polynesian Luau)

- Extensive shopping, dining, nightlife and other activities at Downtown Disney® Area

- Nighttime entertainment on Disney's BoardWalk

- DisneyQuest (A "virtual theme park")

- Even the most veteran Disney traveler can become quickly overwhelmed by the array of offerings and the question of how to allot their budget to make the most magical Disney experience possible. Purchasing this book was your first step toward maximizing the vacation experience you can share with your family in a cost-effective way!

This guide is organized to help you take your hard-earned vacation money and find the experiences that will make your family's vacation goals come true — in affordable, easily understood, and simple-to-implement strategies.

In addition, I have included links to WDW Radio show episodes that will help you, and included fun Walt Disney World trivia to help you appreciate the history and detail you experience while you are in the most Magical Place on Earth!

Let's start by discussing what you can do BEFORE you even leave your home to save money!

102 WAYS
TO SAVE MONEY
FOR AND AT
WALT DISNEY WORLD

BY LOU MONGELLO

BEFORE YOU GO

1   SAVE! Set Up a *"Disney Vacation Savings Account"*
(or a **DIVA — DI**sney **V**acation **A**ccount)

i   Create a separate bank account just for your vacation. Put
away money each week for flights, hotel, souvenirs, etc.
Everyone in the family can participate, by contributing
birthday gift money, holiday gifts, babysitting income, garage
sale earnings, etc.

ii   Find a user-friendly bank. Some banks offer accounts requiring
no minimum balance, have no fees, and have a low initial
deposit minimum to open. Several online banks pay a bit more
interest than a traditional brick and mortar bank, and some
even offer free money if you open a checking account.

iii   Think creatively. Other ways to help fund the account
include:

a.   Sell unused items on eBay

b.   Host a garage sale

c. Develop a coin jar for spare change

d. Reserve a set amount from your paycheck each week for your Disney fund

e. Cash in your tax refund

f. Use coupons. Take the money you saved and put that into your savings account.

g. Distribute piggy banks (not for you, but for the kids!) — Give each child a Disney character piggy bank, so they can start saving on their own. By putting in a few coins in here and there, they will not only learn about saving money, but also feel as though they helped contribute and pay for the family vacation

h. Check out credit card rewards. Both Disney Visa and Discover offer "cash back" opportunities that could be a way to grow a vacation account.

2 **Develop Your Own Payment Plan** — Depending on the type of reservation you have (**package** versus **room-only**), you may not have to pay the full amount when you book your reservation. In many cases, you can make payments at any time to reduce your balance. So, once you book your Walt Disney World room or package, figure out how much time you have from the day you book your reservation until you are required to pay the final payment (a package requires full payment 45 days prior to your arrival. If you are booking room-only, payment of the balance due is made when you check in. You only have to pay one night in advance as a deposit.). Then, at the first of each month (or even after you receive your paycheck), call 1-407-W-DISNEY and make a payment. You can call as many times as you would like to make a payment, (however small it may be), towards your next Disney vacation. Every little bit helps!

3   **Apply for a Disney Rewards Visa** — DisneyRewards.com

i   *You Can Save: Possibly Thousands! Discounts include free dining, up to 40% off at a Walt Disney World Resort, merchandise discounts, and more!*

ii   **No annual fee and great rewards.** Chase Bank (at the time of this writing) offers a no annual fee "Disney Rewards Visa" card that lets you earn 1% in "Disney Dream Reward Dollars®" every time you use your card. So, for every $100 in qualified purchases on the card, you earn 1 Disney Dream Reward Dollar. 1 Disney Dream Reward Dollar is worth $1 when redeemed for Disney products and offerings such as Disney merchandise, park tickets, Disney Resort rooms, dining, etc. at Walt Disney World, Disneyland, the Disney Cruise Line, the Disney Stores and DisneyStore.com.

iii   **Many other perks, including:**

a.   **0% Vacation Financing** — Pay zero interest for 6 months anytime you use your card to book select Disney vacation packages, Disney cruises, Adventures By Disney packages and Aulani vacation packages vacations through the Walt Disney Travel Company, your travel agent, or online at Disney sites. (After your promotional APR expires, your standard purchase APR will apply).

b.   **Theme Park Opportunities**

• Private character meet and greets

- 10% off select merchandise purchases of $50 or more at select Walt Disney World® Resort locations

- 20% off select guided tours (such as Disney's Family Magic Tours, Keys to the Kingdom Tours, Disney's The Magic Behind Our Steam Trains Tour, The UnDISCOVERed Future World, Disney's Dolphins in Depth, and Backstage Safari, among others)

c. **Disney Store** — Use your card and promotion code DRVCMEMBER to save 10% every time you spend $50 or more on qualified purchases at DisneyStore.com and Disney Store retail locations in the US

d. **Disney Cruise Line** — There's nothing better than a "Land and Sea" vacation, combining a Walt Disney World trip and Disney Cruise Line vacation before or after your stay. Disney Rewards Visa cardholders get a $50 onboard credit to use toward shopping, dining, spa treatments and more during their cruise when they book with their card and ask for booking code DCC

e. **0% APR for Disney Vacation Club Financing** — Get 0% APR for 6 months on your Disney Vacation Club down payment or add-on purchase up to $10,000. (Learn more about how Disney Vacation Club ownership can help certain travelers save money in Become a Member! section on page 137)

iv *These offers may vary and are subject to change. Other special offers are often available on the DisneyRewards.com web site, including discounted tickets to Disney's Broadway shows, D23 (D23.com) memberships and more.*

4   Purchase Disney Gift Cards

i   **Buy them!** You can visit your local Disney Store in the mall, at your local Walgreens, or online anytime at <u>DisneyGiftCard. com</u> and purchase a Disney Gift card, which can be used just like cash at any Disney Theme Park and Resort Hotel, on Disney Cruise Line®, and at Disney Stores.

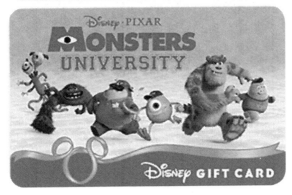

ii   **Add on to them!** Put a little money each week onto the Disney gift card, and by the time you get to Walt Disney World, you can have hundreds of dollars in spending money saved onto the card! You'll find that it's easier to add a small amount each month, rather than trying to save up a large amount of cash to spend or give to your kids while on vacation

iii   **Go online.** You can also reload the cards with additional funds anytime online or even once you get to Walt Disney World

iv   **Gift them.** They also make great gifts and collectibles! You can choose from a number of characters and Disney designs, and each card arrives in a custom holder bearing your personal message.

v   **Request them.** When the holidays or birthdays come around and relatives are asking, *"What can I give the kids?,"* let them know a Disney vacation is being planned and that Disney dollars or a Disney gift card would make a perfect gift!

5   **Purchase Disney Dollars** — as an alternative to Disney gift cards, but with the same mission, you could purchase "Disney dollars" as gifts.

i   Disney Dollars are the official currency of Walt Disney World Resort, the Disneyland Resort and Disney Store locations in the US and Puerto Rico. They are available for purchase denominations of $1, $5 and $10, and each has its own unique Disney Character portraits.

ii   For more information about Disney Dollars, you can call (407) W-DISNEY

iii   You can order Disney Dollars before you arrive at Walt Disney World Resort

   a.   Order by Credit Card — Call (407) 566-4985. Disney Dollars purchased with a credit card are limited to $50 per day and a $15 shipping charge applies

   b.   Order by Cashier's Check or Money Order — Mail your payment and the address to which you wish us to send your order to: P.O. Box 10140, Lake Buena Vista, FL 32830 *(Note that there is a maximum order total of $650 and a $15 shipping charge applies and that check or money orders take 2 weeks for processing).*

   c.   Once you arrive, Disney Dollars can be purchased or exchanged for their equal value in United States currency at Guest Relations at Disney theme parks and water parks or any Disney Resort hotel Front Desk or concierge

6   **Get A Guide** — If you've never been to Walt Disney World before (or even if you have), please don't plan on getting to the resort and just "winging it." You need to plan... and planning is part of the fun! There are many wonderful planning resources and guides, including The Unofficial Guide to Walt Disney World *(Purchase The Unofficial Guide directly from Amazon.com)* and the official Birnbaum's Walt Disney World Guide *(Purchase the Birnbaum Guide directly from Amazon.com)* Because the Birnbaum Guide is the official guide book, it includes coupons in the back of the book for merchandise discounts for some Downtown Disney stores, including:

i   10% off a single purchase at Ridemakerz

ii $10 off a $75 or more purchase at LEGO Imagination Center in Downtown Disney Marketplace in Orlando

iii   10% off all curl by Sammy Duvall merchandise *(except those items which are specifically excluded)*

iv   10% off merchandise at Basin

7   **Join Hilton HHonors™** — You can redeem your Hilton HHonors™ points for tickets to Walt Disney World® and Disneyland® Parks through the HHonors™ Rewards Store. You can also earn additional Hilton HHonors™ points during your vacation by staying at a participating resort near the theme park. hhonors.hilton.com

8   **Don't DO Anything That May Affect You Long-Term** — While a Disney vacation is an amazing experience, avoid negatively affecting long-term financial investments when you are determining how to best plan your vacation.

i   Do NOT charge your vacation on a credit card that you may not be able to pay off in a reasonable time. You should be able to have your vacation paid off within one year.

ii   Do NOT take from your savings account

iii   Do NOT use any "emergency" money

iv   Do NOT withdraw funds (often with a hefty penalty) from any investment, savings, retirement accounts (e.g. 401k, etc.)

9 **Carefully Plan What to Bring from Home (and save money when you are there!)** Thinking carefully about your everyday needs before you leave can save you lots of money in the parks — from avoiding purchasing unnecessary staples to enabling you to plan and use your money wisely in the parks. Make lists for the whole family and plan carefully, remembering toiletries, medications, and clothing for potentially variable weather. Some other items you can bring include:

i **Wipes —** Whether you have a baby or not, moist wipes can be an invaluable resource. From wiping up messy hands after a Mickey ice cream bar to simply bringing a refreshing break to a hot day, these small and easy-to-carry wipes can improve the quality of your day.

ii **Breakfast bars/granola —** If you want to be at the parks first thing in the morning and riding the marquee attractions right away, breakfast "on the go" is an affordable way to use time wisely and keep your energy going! Watch for sales in advance of your trip and pack bars in your suitcases.

iii **Ziploc bags —** Sometimes your children just won't want to eat all their meal, yet are hungry 20 minutes later. If you have a package of Ziploc bags to put the extra grapes or carrots from lunch into, you can break them out when the "I'm hungry" wails begin, and save yourself another line and purchase of a snack.

iv **Sunscreen —** While available in the resort hotels and parks, if you watch for sales back home, you will likely be able to get it more affordably. (Just make sure you don't pack it into your carry-on bag at the airport, as you will have to throw it out!)

v **Laundry Supplies** — If you plan to do laundry while on your vacation, bring a roll of quarters with you. Put some dryer sheets into a ziploc bag and pre-purchase small boxes of detergent. Planning ahead spares you purchasing at a premium in the laundry room.

vi **BYOW** — *Bring Your Own Water* (Bottle) — Bring your own refillable water bottle into the Disney parks and fill it up at any of the many water fountains throughout the day.

vii **Bonus!** — **More Than Just Water** — Want to add a little flavor to your water? Bring single-serve packets of crystal flavors to add to your water bottles — For example, Crystal Light, Kool-Aid for the kids or lemonade crystals. Believe it or not, adding a little bit of fresh, lightly crushed mint leaves to your bottle of water can give it a nice, fresh, taste. Bring some in a zip-top bag and add it to your water bottles! Easy, inexpensive and no artificial sweeteners added!

In 2013, Disney introduced MyMagic+, which will take your vacation to an all-new level, with online and mobile tools to enhance your experience. You can make and share plans before you go, make FASTPASS+ reservations in advance of your trip, connect to your vacation fun with a MyMagic+ band or card, and even personalize your experience! For more information visit http://MyDisneyExperience.com

102 WAYS
TO SAVE MONEY
FOR AND AT
WALT DISNEY WORLD
BY LOU MONGELLO

WHEN TO GO — TIMING IS EVERYTHING

The most important (and potentially biggest) money-saving aspect of your vacation takes place before you go!

10   Evaluate WHEN To Go to Walt Disney World

i   *You Can Save: Thousands!*

ii   **Go "off-season".** Plan your Walt Disney World Resort trip during the "off-season" and you will usually discover significantly lower airfares and hotel/resort rates. Let's discuss what this means to you and your family.

iii   **Track the Disney "seasons."** Like Winter, Summer, Spring, and Fall, Disney has its own "seasons" as well, and by knowing what each offers, you can choose when to visit and save on your Walt Disney World resort hotel stay:

a. *Value Season* is the least expensive and least crowded *(usually January and the first half of February, and then again in the second-half of August and most of September)*

b. *Marathon Rate (only during the Walt Disney World Marathon Weekend, usually in early January)*

c. *Regular Season (end of February-mid March, though this date can be affected by Easter; the month of May)*

d. *Summer Season (June, July, and the first-half of August)*

e. *Fall Season (October, November, and the first 3 weeks of December)*

f. *Peak Season (President's Day weekend, Spring Break/ Easter Weeks)*

g. *Holiday Season (Usually December 23–31)*

iv **Recommended times.** Based upon the seasons of the calendar and the Disney seasons, there are some very desirable times to go that will both save you money AND get the most vacation experience for your dollar.

v **My suggested times to go to Walt Disney World include:**

a. **Mid-November through mid-December (except Thanksgiving week)** — Get the added experience of the holiday decorations, nice weather and some special events without the big holiday crowds. (Weekends may be a bit higher than weekdays)

b. **Mid-January through mid-February** — One of the least busy times of the year, and Disney's resort rates are often at their lowest. It may be cold sometimes, but I have some great ideas for fun things to do when it is cold in Disney! Check out WDW Radio Show 155!

c. **Early to mid-May** — Slightly busier than January and February, and resort rates are traditionally also near the moderate range, but still a great time to go. (Noting that Memorial Day weekend will have larger crowds and possibly higher resort room rates).

d. **End of August through the end of September** — Crowds are usually quite low as the kids (and their parents) get ready to go back to school (Elementary and middle schools also resume sessions in the beginning to middle of August in Florida, so the local crowd will be reduced as well). It will be warm (OK, hot), but that's OK — Disney's resorts have awesome pools and water play areas! Traditionally, Disney has also offered free dining (yes, I said 100% completely FREE dining — see the Dining Section).

11 Save By *Avoiding* Certain Times of the Year

i   *You Can Save: $200.00–$1000.00 Per Week*

ii   **Seasonal times to avoid**. On the other side of the coin, here are some times that, if possible, you may want to avoid:

a. **The week between Christmas and New Years (December 26–31)** — Starting just a few days before Christmas, this is by far the most crowded time of the year. Also, there are usually no discounts offered during this time

b. **The week immediately preceding and following Easter** (from around the middle of February through the first two weeks of April). Right behind Santa, the Easter Bunny (and Spring Break) draws people to Walt Disney World, making it the second busiest time of the year, resulting in high crowds, increased resort prices and even higher airfares across the country.

c. **Summer** — June through the first two weeks of August is prime vacation time for most families, as the kids are out of school. And you don't need to be Nostradamus to know that the weather will be "hot and humid, with continuing hot and humid throughout the week."

d. **"Hurricane Season"** — This time of year runs from about June 1 through November 30, with peaks from mid-August through early October. Be aware that travel during this time may affect the vacation experience

e. **During the Fall...** weekends during the Fall (end of September through mid-December) usually have premium room rates

f. **Holidays and Special Events** — Other busy (and more expensive) times of the year include other US national holidays (Presidents Day, Martin Luther King, Jr. weekend, Labor Day, etc.) and around special events in Walt Disney World (Epcot International Food & Wine Festival, Walt Disney World Marathon Weekend, etc.). Additionally, there are some special offers or discounts that may be blacked out during this time.

iii **Quick Glance Crowd Guide**

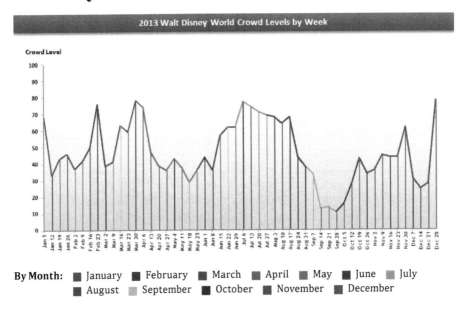

2013 Walt Disney World Crowd Levels by Week

By Month: January February March April May June July August September October November December

a. **Highest Crowds:**

- New Years Day

- Marathon Weekend (usually early January)

- Martin Luther King Holiday Weekend (around January 15)

- Presidents' week (February)

- Mid-March through Late April (Spring Break)

- Easter weekend

- Memorial Day weekend

- Mid-June through Labor Day

- Columbus Day (second Monday of October)

- Thanksgiving Day and weekend

- Christmas week through New Year's Day

b. **Moderate Crowds:**

- From Presidents' week in February through early March

- Late April through early June
  (except Memorial Day weekend)

- The first few days of Thanksgiving week

c. **Lowest Crowds:**

- January *(except New Year's Day)* until just before Presidents' week in February

- The week after Labor Day until just before Thanksgiving week

- The week following Thanksgiving until the week prior to Christmas

d. **Seasonal Note! — Be Aware of Night-by-Night Pricing.** Keep in mind that no matter how long your stay, each night of your vacation is priced separately, so you'll pay the applicable rate for that night's stay. For example, if you check in on the last day of the Holiday Season and the rest of your stay is during the Value Season rate, you'll pay the lower rate for all of the nights outside the Holiday Season. Like I said... timing is everything.

e. **Tip:** An easy guide is to think about times when kids are out of school as traditionally being the most expensive (and crowded) times to visit Walt Disney World. Prices increase with higher demand, so you may spend literally hundreds more per night during the busiest times of year than those that are least busy.

12 Visit During the Weekday

i *You Can Save: $10.00–200.00 Per Night*

ii Rather than start your vacation on a Friday after work or school, begin your vacation on a Sunday, as room rates (and airfare) are typically higher on Friday and Saturday nights. If you can avoid the weekends, you can potentially save hundreds of dollars on your vacation.

13 Get the Most for Your Money — By scheduling your Walt Disney World vacation around one of Disney's annual events and festivals, you can get more "bang for your buck." Many of Disney's annual events are included with the price of admission, including:

i Epcot International Flower & Garden Festival — Epcot is transformed every spring as colorful flowers, lush gardens and Disney character topiaries can be found throughout the park. As a special treat, live musical acts in the Flower Power Concert Series take the stage, and educational programs, event shopping and much more is available for the entire family (usually March through May)

ii   Star Wars Weekends — This annual special event at Disney's Hollywood Studios theme park celebrates the legendary Star Wars Saga and the animated television series, The Clone Wars, with celebrities, special shows, presentations and memorabilia. (usually for four weekends from May-June)

a.   Want to learn more about traveling to Walt Disney World during Star Wars Weekends? Check out these videos and episodes of the WDW Radio Show during which these special weekends are discussed!

- Interview with Ashley Eckstein during Star Wars weekend

- Star Wars Weekend Recap Video

- Show #273: Top Tips to Get the Most Out of Star Wars Weekends and David Prowse (Darth Vader) Interview

- Show #224: Star Tours and Star Wars Weekends and an Interview with Walt Disney Imagineer Kathy Rogers

iii Halloween — For a festive autumn atmosphere, the month of October is a "not so scary" place to enjoy the Halloween spirit. Great decorations add a festive touch. Mickey's Not So Scary Halloween Party (a separate admission ticket event) offers trick or treating and characters in special costumed gear! Check out more fun ways to add a spooky touch to your

Disney vacation by listening to WDW Radio Show #246: Top Ten Spooky Places in Walt Disney World!

iv Epcot International Food & Wine Festival — Held in the Fall, Epcot is transformed into a food and wine lover's paradise with dozens of specialty food kiosks with flavors from around the world, culinary events, seminars and (free!) live musical entertainment. (usually around late September through the middle of November) The EPCOT International Food and Wine Festival is near and dear to my heart (and stomach!) To hear more about this event, check out these videos and episodes of the WDW Radio Show!

    a. Video: Epcot International Food & WIne Festival: Top Five Flavors

    b. Video: Walt Disney World Swan & Dolphin Food & Wine Classic

    c. Show #245: An On-Location Review of the 2012 International Food and Wine Festival

    d. Show #243: Learn more about the Swan and Dolphin Food & Wine Classic and EPCOT's Party for the Senses.

    e. Show #194: A Roundtable Review of the 2011 Epcot International Food & Wine Festival*

v   Festival of the Masters — This open-air art festival is held in autumn at Downtown Disney and features more than 150 award-winning artists.

vi Holiday Season — The Disney parks' seasonal displays, shows and special events, including Holidays Around the World and the Osborne Family Spectacle of Dancing Lights make it truly the most wonderful time of the year to visit (usually from the end of November through the end of December)

a. This video will provide you with an overview of Christmas and the Holidays at Walt Disney World.

b. Learn more about Thanksgiving in Walt Disney World by listening to WDW Radio Show #146: How to spend a traditional holiday in a non-traditional location!

DID YOU KNOW? For 17 years, Walt Disney World presented a live nativity display called The Glory and Pageantry of Christmas. It ran at the Disney Village Marketplace (now called DownTown Disney) and came to an end in 1994.

14 **Monitor Vacation Discounts from Disney** — Disney itself offers a number of discounts and special offers throughout the year. These offers vary seasonally and often may come as an unexpected surprise. Sometimes, Disney sends out special offers to guests via postcard or email with personal PIN codes. These codes can be used when booking a Walt Disney World vacation and offer great discounts on rooms and vacation packages. You can't request or transfer PIN codes as they are generated specifically for you. Current offers available to the general public can always be found by visiting Disney's web site at DisneyWorld.com

i   *You Can Save: Up to 10%–30% Off Rack Rates*

ii   If you have an upcoming conference at Walt Disney World, go ahead and plan a family vacation around it! Attending a conference allows you extra discounts and perks that are not available to the general public, including half-day tickets and meal vouchers. For those attending the convention, there are also a variety of discounted ticket options as well:

iii   **Meeting/Convention Tickets** — These tickets are for sale and use ONLY by individuals attending a meeting or convention in Central Florida and their companions during their stay. The tickets will be valid for use only during the convention/meeting times, and for a day or two before and after as determined by Disney. The tickets also expire 14 days after first use, which has to be within 7 days after the end of the applicable meeting or convention. For more information, contact your event organizer or visit DisneyConventionears.Disney.go.com/ or DisneyDestinationsTickets.com

iv   **Partial-Day Tickets** There is also an "After 2pm" and "After 4pm" Meeting/Convention Ticket which allows you to catch up with your family and enjoy the parks after your meetings have ended.

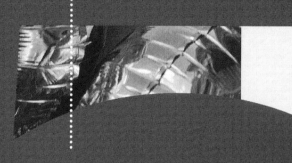

102
WAYS
TO SAVE MONEY
FOR AND AT
WALT DISNEY WORLD

BY LOU MONGELLO

HOW TO GO — USING TRAVEL AGENTS, BOOKING AIRFARE, AND FINDING CARS!

MAKING YOUR DISNEY RESERVATION

16   Use a Travel Agent... for Free!

i   *You Can Save: $300-500 Per Week! (Finding discount codes, booking room and tickets separately, saving you time and hassle etc.)*

AUTHORIZED DISNEY VACATION PLANNER

©Disney

ii   Did you know that you could book your travel through an Authorized Disney Vacation Planner at no additional cost to you? You pay the same (and in many cases, lower) rates than you would if you book directly with a supplier. The travel agencies are compensated by the travel suppliers who pay them commissions on their sales. *(I personally recommend and use* *http://MouseFanTravel.com). By booking* with an Authorized Disney Vacation Planner, you also receive a number of additional benefits:

a. **Free Travel Planning Advice and Services** — Complimentary, concierge-style service is often offered. As part of their planning services, most Authorized Disney Vacation Planners will make your advanced dining reservations, help schedule special events, offer insights on additional experiences, or just provide friendly advice to make your vacation magical. This is a HUGE benefit over trying to book through an online supplier, where you often cannot speak to someone directly who can answer your questions or make special arrangements. Also, many sites, such as Expedia, don't always offer room-only reservations, , instead requiring you to book a package that includes your hotel and theme park tickets. Your Authorized Disney Vacation Planner should be able to customize your trip to your needs and requirements.

b. **Dedicated Agent** — most agencies (like Mouse Fan Travel), will assign you a specific travel planner who will guide you through the entire process, and be there to answer questions, make changes, or help if needed.

c. **Best Price Possible** — Your agent should continually and proactively check for discounts and apply any savings for which your booking will qualify without you having to ask.

d. **Group Planning** — Bringing the whole family? Extended family? A large group? Your travel agent can help with planning special events, dining and other experiences to ensure everyone has a truly "magical" time!

17   Become a Member of AAA

i   *You Can Save: 10–20% at a Walt Disney World Resort*

ii   Membership DOES Have Its Privileges!! If you are a member of the American Automobile Association (**AAA**), you may be able to take advantage of special rates or discounts that are available for your Walt Disney World vacation. From theme park tickets to resort rooms and full packages, AAA members can often find discounted rates by visiting AAA.com When booking a AAA Vacation Package, you will enjoy some additional benefits, including (these are subject to change. Check AAA.com for current offers and details):

iii   **Preferred viewing** location for the Wishes™ Nighttime Spectacular in Magic Kingdom® Theme Park.

iv   **An exclusive Disney's Story Time Experience** — If you purchase select AAA Vacations packages that include a Disney Dining Plan, you may be able to enjoy a special storytelling experience featuring a classic Disney animated film character in Epcot®

v   **AAA Vacations Diamond Savings Card** — This special card offers savings and values from 10% to 20% off at many participating dining, recreation, merchandise, tour, and spa locations throughout the Walt Disney World Resort

vi   **AAA Diamond Parking** — Preferred Parking spaces are available (limited availability) at all four Walt Disney World Theme Parks

vii   **AAA Vacations Keepsake Luggage Tag** (one per person).

18   **Analyze the Need for Trip Insurance.**

i   Purchasing comprehensive trip insurance through a reputable company is the best way to protect your trip and to have complete peace of mind in the event illness, weather, or another unexpected event interferes with your vacation plans at the last minute. Considering how much you may be spending on your vacation, it's worth it to protect your investment. I especially recommend trip insurance when traveling during peak hurricane season.

ii   If you book through an Authorized Disney Vacation Planner, they can discuss the coverage with you and help obtain a travel insurance quote. If you book your own travel, you can visit InsureMyTrip.com or TravelGuard.com for rates and information.

FLYING TO DISNEY

DID YOU KNOW? Eastern Airlines was the first "official" airline of WDW and sponsored one of the Magic Kingdom's early attractions, *If You Had Wings.* Delta airlines also was the official airline of Walt Disney World, although at this time, there is no official airline.

19   **Book Your Airfare Early**

i   *You Can Save: Hundreds!*

ii   Try booking your flights as early as possible, with 4 months apparently being an ideal time. (Airlines don't start releasing cheaper seats until 3–4 months before departure for domestic travel). If you purchase your tickets more than 21 days in advance, you will likely find much better rates than if you book closer to your departure date.

20 Book Your Flight Online

ii Booking your air travel online enables you not only to search and compare fares, but also to avoid waiting on hold for an agent. More importantly, many of the airlines offer discounts when booking your tickets online through their specific web sites. By booking on an airline's site directly, you will also avoid the service fees that many of the airlines have started to charge. For example, some airlines charge a $5 fee for booking over the phone, and between $5 to $10 for booking in person at ticket offices and airport counters.

iii   **Extra Savings:** *You Can Save: Up to $125 per Ticket*

> If there is a possibility that you will need to change your flight, book directly with the airline, as some sites like Orbitz.com and Travelocity.com charge an additional fee (around $30) to change a flight, in addition to whatever change fees the airline itself may impose (sometimes between $25 and $150 *per ticket*, depending on the airline).

21   **Check the Major Sites** — In addition to the major airlines' sites, be sure to check some of the large online travel sites, as they have negotiated bulk pricing with the airlines. Some recommended sites include Travelocity.com, Cheapflights.com, Orbitz.com and Expedia.com. By searching and comparing, you can also see which of their package deals that combine flights, hotel and car rentals can save you the most money (and are pretty convenient as well).

i   **Orbitz Price Assurance** — Once you book on Orbitz.com, they will start tracking to see if another Orbitz customer subsequently books the same flight or hotel reservation on Orbitz.com at a lower price. If that happens, they will issue a refund for the difference. Amounts range from $5 to $250 per airline ticket or $5 to $500 per hotel room. They continue tracking until the day you leave, so each time the price drops and another customer subsequently books your same itinerary for a lower amount, your refund amount will increase. Refund checks are mailed approximately 6–8 weeks after your trip is complete, and then you have the start of a new "Disney fund!"

ii   **Comparison Shop** — Kayak.com is different than the other search sites. Although it is a search engine for flights, hotels and rental cars, Kayak does not actually sell tickets. It's the aggregate all of the travel sites so you can compare prices from all of the major vendors. It's the first stop I make when booking air travel or looking for packages online.

22   **Sign up for Fare Alerts** — Many airlines (like Southwest's "Ding" service Southwest.com/ding), as well as sites like FareCompare.com, Orbitz, Expedia and Travelocity, allow you to sign up online (for free) to be notified about deals on specific routes or destinations. Tuesdays at 3:00pm seems traditionally to be the time when the best fares are available, so be ready! Why? Because airlines usually launch sales late Monday, which means that other airlines start lowering prices to compete, and by Tuesday afternoon, the greatest opportunity to find the best prices is available.

23   **Check Out Auction Sites** — If you can be flexible in your travel plans or dates (and don't mind — or even like! — a little "adventure" in your planning), look at some of the auction or discount sites like Priceline.com and Hotwire.com. Each offers airline tickets at deeply discounted prices, but there's a catch: You can't select your specific flight times and you won't even know what airline you're booking on until AFTER you buy your ticket.

i   *You Can Save: Up to 50% off per Ticket*

ii   Hotwire.com — Enter in your destination and travel dates and Hotwire.com returns the best fare it can find for that route. You'll have only one hour to accept the price and buy the ticket. Otherwise the deal expires and you'll have to wait another 48 hours before you can make the same request. Check the Hotwire.com web site to see what air carriers are their current partners.

iii   Priceline.com — Put in where you want to go, when you want to go and what you're willing to pay, and Priceline. com will let you know if your offer has been accepted by an airline. It is VERY important to note, however, that if your price and itinerary has been accepted, your credit card will immediately be charged.

iv   **Bonus Tip:** Try looking for an offer on Hotwire.com, then bid a little bit lower on Priceline. If Priceline rejects your offer, you can still go back to Hotwire.com (within 60 minutes) and take their offer. Remember that tickets purchased on both sites are non-refundable, and if your travel plans change, your ticket cannot be changed.... no, not even at an additional cost! Also, you will NOT earn frequent flyer miles for flights booked on these sites.

24   Travel on a Weekday

i   *You Can Save: Up to 50% off Per Ticket*

ii   Tuesdays, Wednesdays and Thursdays are usually the least expensive days to fly. You may get the occasional discounted fare on a Saturday, but traditionally it's more expensive to fly on a weekend than a weekday. Also, airfare sales (traditionally) tend to occur early in the week, and increases normally occur at the end of the week. Keep in mind that domestic airlines can (and do) sometimes change fares up to three times a day on weekdays, and once a day on weekends. That's another good reason to sign up for fare alerts (see above). When you see a good deal — grab it!

25   Remember: **Timing is everything...** so be as flexible as you can in your travel times. Traveling before 8:00 a.m. or on overnight

flights (the "red-eye"), will usually help save on airfare. Your kids may not want to get up that early, but it's much easier when they know they're going to Walt Disney World!

26   **Be Flexible in Your Travel Dates** — When searching for flights, look to depart and return a day or two before or after your proposed dates, as many airline websites will show you the cheapest flights available within a window of dates.

27   **Know when to look and book** — Most sale fares show up on Monday around 8 p.m., and end on Thursday at 8 p.m., so buying your tickets at 3:00 p.m. on a Tuesday may give you your best deal, according to FareCompare.com

28   **Check Nearby Airports**

i   *You Can Save: Hundreds of Dollars*

ii   You may be able to get a better deal by driving a bit farther and save hundreds of dollars by leaving from an alternate airport than the one that is closest to your home. Most online travel sites allow you to search nearby airports, and this can provide a substantial savings. For a family of four, driving or taking a taxi for a few extra miles could add up to big savings. For example, if the airfare to Sanford International Airport (SFB) is $75 per ticket less than flying into Orlando International Airport (MCO), a family of four can save $300 in airfare alone. Orlando International is approximately 24 miles (30 minutes) away from Walt Disney World, while Sanford is only 48 miles (50 minutes) away. Not only that, but smaller airports like Sanford are generally less crowded, let you get your luggage faster, have fewer flight delays, and quick, easy access to rental cars.

29 **Consider a Layover.** Making one or two brief layovers usually will reduce the cost of your flight significantly. Yeah, it's a bit more of a hassle when traveling with small children, but it could save you hundreds of dollars (that you can use in the parks)!

30 **Make it a Weekend!** — Most low fare deals require staying over a Saturday night before your return flight. However, some fares may only require you to stay a minimum of 3 or 4 days.

31 **Use a Travel Agent To Book Your Flights** — Travel agents can also help find a travel package or flights for you, especially when you are looking to book air travel that may have multiple stops, international flights, etc. They can also save you time (and time IS money, right?) looking at alternatives like nearby airports, finding available discounts, booking as part of a group, helping with changes or cancellations, and confirming everything is as you had planned and requested. And don't be afraid to just ask... Sometimes there may be available discounts that you don't know about (for example, if you are active military personnel, seniors 65 and older, students, etc.).

32 **Use Miles**

   i *You Can Save: The Full Cost of a Plane Ticket*

   ii If you have rewards points or frequent flier miles, use them to help reduce costs for your trip to Walt Disney World. Keep in mind that the airlines designate a very limited number of seats on each flight as eligible for award travel, and these seats often go very quickly. Look and book early!

33 Bring Carry-on Luggage Only

i *You Can Save: $25 per person (or more!)*

ii Since many airlines are now charging up to $25 for just the first bag, bring only a carry-on bag and personal item (backpack, purse, etc.)

34 Bring Your Own Food

i *You Can Save: $5–10 per person, depending on the snack you would have purchased on the plane*

ii The days of the airlines providing meals for coach class seem to be over, and the limited meal packs they offer on board are often very expensive. Bring food from home! Even items purchased in the airport can be less expensive than those bought on the plane. I often bring re-sealable packs of granola, nuts, dried fruits, etc. (and usually some chocolate... just in case). Also, if possible, be sure to eat before you get to the airport, or make a sandwich (minus any liquid condiments) at home and bring it with you.

iii **Drink for Free** — Bring an empty water bottle to the airport and once you get through security, fill it at a water fountain for free.

35 Bump Me!!!

i *You Can Save: Up to $400*

ii I recommend this only if traveling solo or as a couple — Airlines often overbook flights and offer a place on a later flight for those willing to give up their seat. They will often also offer you a travel voucher or credit (sometimes up to $350–400) on your next flight. If your travel plans are flexible, this is a great way to save on your next trip! If you get to the gate early, you can ask the agent if there is a possibility to get bumped.

DRIVING TO AND IN DISNEY

To Drive or not to drive... To Rent a car... or don't...

36 **Don't Rent a Car!**

i *You Can Save: Hundreds of Dollars Per Week*

ii You don't need one. If you're staying in a Walt Disney World resort, you don't NEED a car — transportation is provided for free via buses, monorail system, and a variety of cool (and fun!) watercraft. If you fly into Orlando International Airport (MCO) and are staying at a Walt Disney World Resort, free bus transportation is provided to and from the airport via Disney's Magical Express.

37 **Rent a Car... and Save!** If You Want a Car, Here Are Some Money-Saving Tips:

i *You Can Save: Up to 50%*

ii **Check car rental web sites** — often — for discounts. Believe it or not, prices can change daily, so keep trying for lower rates all the time. Alamo.com (the official rental car company of Walt Disney World) has great rates, and a location on property if you need to rent a car there or if you have any difficulties with your rental during your stay. They also have a rental location inside the Orlando International Airport.

iii **Join the rental car company's membership/frequent renter program.** These programs are often free and can offer additional discounts. Also compare rates from the car rental company's web site, their 1-800 number and their local office, as you may be able to get better pricing from one over the other.

iv **Book Early!** — The least expensive cars often book up fastest, so once you know your travel dates, start looking in to reserving your vehicle rental.

v **Use Other Discounts.**

    a. Do you belong to AAA, AARP or a wholesale club like Costco? Often times they have discounts or rebates on car rentals. Inquire with your organization, or ask when you book with the rental car company if these discounts are available.

    b. Now is the time to scour all your frequent flier clubs, credit cards, entertainment coupon books, and membership organizations for discounts on car rentals. Even a 10 percent discount or $35 rebate off a weekly rental will help to offset rising rental car costs.

vi **Avoid the Airport** — While picking up your car from a rental company with a location in the terminal is convenient, you can often save by renting a car from an off-site company. This will allow you to avoid some additional airport and other fees. Most companies have a free shuttle to their nearby rental location.

vii **Shorter (or Longer) is Better!** Rent for less than 3 days or for more than 5 for the best prices and offers, as sometimes renting for a longer period of time will get you a better per-day deal.

viii **Stay a Saturday.** Lower rates are often available if your rental term includes an overnight stay over a Saturday night.

ix **Skip the Rental Insurance** — Read the policies yourself carefully, and use your own judgment, but chances are you won't need the additional renter's insurance from the car rental companies. Inquire with your personal auto insurance company to see if their coverage will extend to a rental car.

x **Fill 'Er Up —** *You Can Save: $3 Per Gallon (or $48 Per Tank of Gas)* — Be sure you fill up on gas before returning your car to the rental location or airport, or they'll charge you a fortune for each gallon of gas (sometimes as high as $7.00 per gallon).

38 **Know How to** *Really* **Save on Gas!** Fill up **in** Walt Disney World. Am I crazy? Not at all. In fact, gas prices are often less expensive at the Hess stations on Walt Disney World property. There are currently three Hess stations on property:

i **Near the Magic Kingdom on World Drive —** Open 24 hours a day, it includes a 4,000 square foot convenience store, car care center for repairs, and rental car office for Alamo or National. Shuttle service is provided from the Disney resorts.

ii **Across from Downtown Disney —** Open 24 hours, it has a small convenience store as well

iii **Located across from Disney's Hollywood Studios and Disney's Boardwalk Resort —** Open 24 hours, it has self-service gas, car wash, and a convenience store

iv **Map to nearby gas stations:** WDWRadio.com/Gas

39 **Getting there IS Half the Fun! —** Are you driving to Walt Disney World (like my family and I did every year from New Jersey)? There are ways to save on gas as well:

i **Mobile Device Apps —** There are several (FREE!) apps for your mobile devices that can help you find gas stations with the least expensive prices. Check your device's app store, but also look at these free options:

a. AAA Trip Tik Mobile (free): Has maps and directions, hotel and restaurant information, directions, and gas station locations showing current fuel prices.

b. Gasbuddy (free): Locate gas stations near you and see their current gas prices.

c. Cheap Gas (free): Get a list of stations, sorted in order of the lowest price. Tap a listing and it opens Maps which shows your current location and that of the station you selected (no directions provided)

ii **Amtrak Auto Train** — The Amtrak Auto Train transports you and your car (or your van, motorcycle, or SUV) nonstop from the Washington, DC area to Sanford, Florida, not far from Walt Disney World. It's a great way to make (or avoid) the drive down I-95. Pack your car as if it were your suitcase, and then sit back and relax in your roomy coach seat or reserve a private Bedroom or Roomette. Better yet, you can save 900 miles of driving, gasoline and wear and tear on your car. For more information and for rates, visit Amtrak. com/auto-train

102
WAYS
TO SAVE MONEY
FOR AND AT
WALT DISNEY WORLD

BY LOU MONGELLO

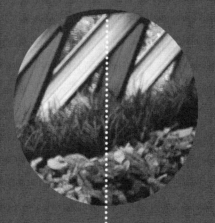

TICKETS — CHOOSING THE RIGHT OPTION CAN SAVE YOU MONEY AND LET YOU DO MORE FOR LESS

DID YOU KNOW? When the Magic Kingdom opened in 1971, guests didn't get in for a flat fee. Each attraction (with the exception of a few freebies) required a ticket, and guests purchased ticket books containing A, B, C, D, and E tickets. The best attractions required E tickets. In the early 1980's, in anticipation of the opening of "EPCOT Center," the ticket books were phased out and replaced with "Passports" that offered guest admission and unlimited access to the attractions.

Choosing the best Walt Disney World ticket option will be based on a number of factors, and can help you save money (and frustration) during your trip. When selecting what works best for your family, take into consideration how long you'll be at Walt Disney World, your budget, and how your family travels and vacations. Keep in mind you will want time to sit back, relax, and enjoy your time at the parks and resorts as well. Considering that your Walt Disney World Theme Park tickets may be one of your largest expenses, deciding which option is right for you and your family is one of the most important decisions you need to make.

40 **Plan your trip to be 6–7 days long. (a longer trip really IS better!) Set realistic expectations.** OK, let's establish one fact right off the bat: no matter how long your Walt Disney World vacation may be, you will not be able to see and do it all. With 4 parks, 2 water parks, shopping, dining, entertainment and more, there's just not enough time for everything. (Which is a great reason to keep coming back!). That being said, you CAN do a lot in a short amount of time, but I recommend your vacation be 6–7 days long. And believe it or not, **the longer you stay, the more money you will save!**

i   **Ticketing Basics — *You Can Save: More Than 50%... or up to $1000!*** Disney offers flexible ticket options that let you choose the ticket or pass that's right for you. "Magic Your Way" Base Tickets give each member of your travel party entry to one Theme Park per day for each day of your ticket. And now "the longer you play, the less you pay per day!"

a.   Depending on length of ticket purchased, the average price per day for a 7-day Magic Your Way Base Ticket is *less than half* the price of the same single-day ticket. It's like saving over 50%!

b. Practically speaking, tickets are heavily discounted on longer (5 to 7 day) stays. So a 7-day ticket costs just a bit more than a 4 day ticket. So don't think that you can only afford a long weekend or 4-day vacation. Check the pricing for a week-long trip and you'll be pleasantly surprised at the cost differences. In most cases, a family of 4 can **save more than $1000.00** by taking one longer vacation rather than 2 shorter ones.

ii **Ticket Options** — In addition to choosing the number of days (from 1 to 10) of your ticket, you can add some options in any combination you choose:

a. **Park Hopper Option** — With this add-on, you can come and go through each of the four Walt Disney World theme parks on the same day for the entire length of your ticket. This option runs about $55 per person, no matter how many days are on your Magic Your Way Ticket.

b. **Water Park Fun & More Option** — Includes visits to your choice of Disney's Blizzard Beach Water Park, Disney's Typhoon Lagoon Water Park, DisneyQuest Indoor Interactive Theme Park, ESPN Wide World of Sports Complex or Disney's Oak Trail Golf Course *(with reserved tee time)*. This option runs about $55 and the number of visits depends on number of days purchased on a Magic Your Way Ticket. For example, if you have a four-day ticket, the Water Park Fun & More Option is $55 and gives you a total of four visits to the water parks and other recreation areas. If you have a ten-day ticket, you get ten recreation visits for the same price of $55.

c. **No Expiration Option** — Magic Your Way Base Tickets expire 14 days from their first use, unless the No Expiration Option is added. With this option, your unused Theme Park days and Water Park Fun & More visits never expire. This option is not available on one-day tickets, and the cost varies depending on length of ticket. This adds some peace of mind knowing that if for some reason you don't use some days on your ticket (maybe you want to relax at the resort, etc.) you ensure that any unused days will be available for your next visit.

iii **Bonus Tip:** Take a photo of the back of each of your theme park admission tickets. This way, if any of the tickets gets lost, you can easily reference the number on the back and have it replaced at any Guest Relations location. This will be the only way to get tickets replaced that may get lost on your trip. For tickets purchased at Walt Disney World, keep ticket receipts in a safe place. This can also help get missing tickets replaced.

41   **Make a Decision: To Hop or Not To Hop (PS: There's no wrong choice!)**

i   *Don't Park Hop! — You Can Save: $440.00*

For a family of four, visiting one theme park per day and not park hopping between them can save you around $440!

ii   **Start Hopping!** — Then again, there are some reasons why you SHOULD get the Park Hopping option:

a.   If you are on the Disney Dining Plan, the park hopper option may be a good choice. Why? Let's say you're spending the day in the Magic Kingdom, but it's also the only day that you could get reservations at Le Cellier in Epcot. In this case, the park hopper enables you to have the best of both worlds.

b.   **The nice thing is — You Can Change Your Mind!** If you choose the Base Tickets and then decide to add the Park Hopper option on, you can — even after your trip has started! You can go to Guest Relations at any Walt Disney World Theme Park and add it on if you feel that you need it.

42   **Be wary of "Discount" Tickets** — If it sounds too good to be true, chances are it is! "Discounted" tickets are not always what they seem to be, and for many reasons, I recommend never (ever) buying Walt Disney World Theme Park tickets on eBay, Craigslist and other online sites. Additionally, I suggest you not be lured in by the big signs alongside the road promising highly discounted tickets. Many of them are scams. Those that are legitimate usually require a long (very long) trip to a timeshare sales pitch that can last hours.

43 **Use Military Discounts** — Disney salutes the men and women from the armed forces, both active and retired, as well as Department of Defense civilian employees and their dependents by offering discounted tickets for them and their families.

i *You Can Save: 6.5% (Florida Tax)*

ii Tickets are available at the Shades of Green resort in Walt Disney World or at a military base (MWR/ITT office). Best of all — they are tax-free! A local Navy Exchange in Orlando is located near the Orlando International Airport on Earhart Drive. Call (407) 857-3550 for more information.

iii The tickets can also be purchased at any theme park ticket window or at Guest Relations in Downtown Disney, **but** tax will be added at those locations if you do so.

iv These tickets are available ONLY for active or retired members of the US military, including the National Guard, Reservists and the US Coast Guard, with a valid military ID card.

v Learn how you can also save by staying at a special, military-only Walt Disney World Resort!

vi Be sure to mention your military status to your travel agent, as they may be aware of other offers that are sometimes released.

vii Check with Shades of Green and DisneyWorld.com for special military salute tickets and other offers.

44 **Ask if Your Company May Be Able to Help!** —

i **Corporate Sponsors** — Some companies that have a business relationship with Disney (including corporate sponsors, etc.) may offer their employees discounted theme park tickets. Check with your Human Resources department for more information.

ii **Large Corporations** — Other large corporations may also offer discounted tickets, even though no specific sponsorship relationship may exist. Check with your HR department for information and availability.

45 Participate in Disney's Y.E.S. (Youth Education Services) Program

i *You Can Save: Up to 50% Off Tickets*

ii Disney Youth Education Series is a program that includes more than 25 field studies that take place within the Disney Parks. Programs are designed for students in first through twelfth grades and focus on science, animation, the arts, history, leadership and careers. Others are tailored to the needs of college students.

iii Registered classes or groups are eligible to purchase discounted tickets from 3-Day to 10-Day Base Tickets, with the optional Park Hopper and Water Park Fun & More options.

iv **Bonus Tip:** While the Y.E.S. program is primarily designed for classes and groups, there are some "individual enrollment" opportunities that may be available to individual students. Learn more: DisneyYouth.com/ individual-enrollment

46   Become an Annual Passholder!

i   *You Can Save: Thousands!!*

ii   **Join the club!** By becoming a Walt Disney World Annual Passholder, you get unlimited admission and park hopping to all four Walt Disney World Theme Parks, as well as exclusive events and great discounts on select options including dining, merchandise, recreation, tours and more!

iii   *"But I'm only going once this year."* — Believe it or not, if you plan on visiting Walt Disney World and staying more than 7or 8 days in a 365-day span, an Annual Pass may be a great way to save! And, by timing your vacations just right, if you visit Walt Disney World every year, you can REALLY save! How?

    a. *Here's an example:* If you vacation every summer and visit Walt Disney World during the last week of July for a few days, you can purchase your Annual Pass and use it on that trip.

    b. The following year, you schedule your visit during the first two weeks of July and use the same Annual Pass, meaning your tickets for next year's trip are already paid for!

    c. Using this tip, you will save hundreds (or depending on the size of your family, thousands!) of dollars!

iv   *"But I want to go to the water parks, too!"* — No problem! By purchasing a Premium Annual Pass, you get unlimited access *(except activities/events separately priced)* to: both Disney water parks, Disney's Oak Trail Golf Course, DisneyQuest Indoor Interactive Theme Park, and ESPN Wide World of Sports complex *(Valid only on event days)*

v   **Save on Your Resort Rooms Reservation** — As an Annual or Seasonal Passholder, you not only save on the cost of your tickets but you can also get additional (deep) discounts on your Walt Disney World Resort rooms as well — sometimes as much as 45% off the "rack" rate!

vi   **Save on Merchandise, too!**

   a. *You Can Save: 10–20% on Merchandise*

   b. That's right! An Annual Pass can save the Passholder 10-20% on most merchandise items on Walt Disney World property. Premium Annual Passholders can receive a 20% discount and all other Annual Passholders are entitled to a 10% discount on select merchandise purchases at Walt Disney World Resort owned and operated merchandise locations. Even on low-priced souvenirs, using your Annual Pass can add up to big savings over the course of your trip! Check here for more information: Walt Disney World Annual Passholder Merchandise Discounts

c. Note that the discount is not valid on purchases of some items, such as tickets, gift certificates, Disney Gift Cards, DVD's and CD's, Disney Dollars, digital and video cameras, Disney's PhotoPass products, certain collectibles (such as original art, handmade items which are physically touched by an artist or vendor), and other select merchandise.

d. Note also that according to the terms of use, the discount is for personal use only and may not be used to purchase merchandise with the intent to resell the merchandise. Ask a Cast Member and consult your Annual Pass guidelines for more information

vii **Save on Experiences**

a. ***You Can Save: 10–50% off Sports & Recreation***

b. You can also save on many additional Sports and Recreational Activities as well, including (but not limited to):

- 10% off Bass Nitro Fishing and Guided Fishing Excursions

- 50% off Disney's Fantasia Gardens Miniature Golf Course and Disney's Winter Summerland Miniature Golf Course for the annual passholder and up to 3 Guests.

- 30% off golfing on the Day Visitor Rates at the Walt Disney World Championship Courses, available for the Passholder and up to 3 Guests in the party.

- 15% off marina boat rentals at any Walt Disney World Resort marina, including Specialty Fireworks Cruises. *Certain age restrictions apply (excludes Holiday Event Specialty Cruises and the Grand 1 Yacht).*

- 10% off the Richard Petty Driving Experience: Ride-Along or Driving Experience package.

- 10% off at Sammy Duvall's Water Sports Centre on Parasailing, Water-Skiing, Wakeboarding, and personal watercraft at Sammy Duvall's Water Sports Centre at Disney's Contemporary Resort for the Passholder after 12:00 noon.

viii **Spas and Salons — You Can Save: 10% off Your Spa Treatment**

   a. Annual Passholders can save 10% on one regularly priced, 50-minute spa treatment per visit at the Walt Disney World Massage & Fitness Centers located at: Disney's Animal Kingdom Lodge, Disney's Boardwalk Inn Resort, Disney's Contemporary Resort, Disney's Coronado Springs Resort, Disney's Wilderness Lodge, Disney's Yacht & Beach Club Resorts, The Spa & Health Club at Disney's Saratoga Springs Resort & Spa

   b. Annual Passholders can also save 10% on one regularly priced salon treatment of $45.00 or greater per visit at: Disney's Contemporary Resort Salon, Disney's Coronado Springs Resort Salon, and Disney's Yacht & Beach Club Resorts Salon

ix Save on your rental car!

   a. **You Can Save: 20% On Your Rental Car**

   b. Annual Passholders who rent from Alamo® Rent A Car can save up to 20% on your rental by reserving online or calling Alamo directly.

x   **And there's more!** — Consult your *Mickey Monitor,* the collectible, Passholder-only publication that is sent regularly to those with an annual pass, which may include additional discounts or coupons.

xi **You should get an Annual Pass... but you may not need one for the entire family —** *You Can Save: 15–20% On Your Resort Stay!*

    a. What? It's true! In order to take advantage of Annual Passholder discounts on rooms and merchandise, only ONE person in the room needs to have an Annual Pass!

    b. So let's say you're only taking one vacation within a 365-day period of time, and it's only for a few days. It certainly doesn't make sense for everyone in the family or group to get an Annual Pass, right? But if the savings on the room (and don't forget the merchandise discounts of 10% off for Annual Passholders, and 20% off for Premium Annual Passholders) make sense versus the rack rate, you may be able to save a great deal of money by having an Annual Pass.

xii And don't forget that Annual Passholders are also entitled to purchase the Tables in Wonderland Discount Dining Card — *You Can Save: 20% on Dining*

a. For just $100 for Passholders and $125 for Florida residents, you will save 20% at most table-service restaurants (including alcohol!) in Walt Disney World. So by having one person in your group purchasing an Annual Pass, the ENTIRE group will save on resort rooms, meals and alcohol and merchandise! (The Tables in Wonderland discount applies to a party of up to 10 guests, including the card holder.)

b. You can also save on merchandise, not just in the parks, but the resorts and Downtown Disney!

- Passholder discounts at Disney-owned-and-operated locations at the Walt Disney World Resort are currently:

- 20% off for Premium Annual Passholders and Premier Passholders (see Tip #47 to learn more about the Premier Passport) and 10% off for all other Passholders

- Passholder discounts are also available for some locations owned and operated by operating participants in Downtown Disney and Animal Kingdom, including:

  - 10% off at Arribas Brothers,Basin, Curl by Sammy Duvall, House of Blues store, LEGO Imagination Center, and Planet Hollywood store

  - 15% off at LittleMissMatched, Rainforest Cafe shops at Downtown Disney and Animal Kingdom locations, T-REX Cafe Dino-Store, Yak & Yeti Bhaktapur Market in Disney's Animal Kingdom Park

xiii But wait! There's more! As an Annual Passholder, you get discounts on Disney's Tours as well

   a. ***You Can Save: 15% on Tours & Experiences***

   b. Each Passholder can get 15% off many of the Tours and Experiences available. For information and reservations call (407) WDW-TOUR (939-8687). (Valid for Passholder only)

xiv **Disney's Best Kept Secret**... Shhhh.... Did you know that Disney Vacation Club Members ALSO receive discounts on Annual and Premium Annual Passes? Members can contact Member Services or visit the DVC web site and check on discounts that can be between $90 and $125 off per pass (depending on adult or child, regular vs. Premium)!

47 **Purchase The Best of the Best** — Disney's Premier Passport:

i If you are a fan of Disney Parks on both coasts, you can get a year of admission to both Disneyland Resort theme parks in Anaheim, and the 4 theme parks and 2 water parks at Walt Disney World Resort in Orlando with a Disney Premier Passport. It's the ultimate Disney Parks experience ticket!

ii The Premier Passport allows access to both east coast and west coast resort parks with no blackout dates for one year. Passholders will also be able to visit multiple parks on the same day, as well as get unlimited admission to Typhoon Lagoon and Blizzard Beach, DisneyQuest Indoor Interactive Theme Park, ESPN Wide World of Sports Complex (with restrictions) and Disney's Oak Trail Golf Course (with restrictions). The pass also includes free theme park parking and a subscription to *Mickey Monitor* and *Backstage Pass*.

iii   If you are already an Annual Passholder, you can upgrade your annual or seasonal pass for one resort to a Disney Premier Passport by visiting Disneyland Resort theme park ticket booths; Guest Relations windows at Walt Disney World theme parks; and Downtown Disney area at Walt Disney World Resort.

48   Renew Your Annual Pass!

i   *You Can Save: $50.00*

ii   As if the Annual Pass discounts weren't enough, you can also save on your pass when renewing it!! If you renew your pass up to 30 days after your "Anniversary Date" (the day your Pass was activated), you will receive a renewal discount of around $50 per pass (subject to change). For more information, visit here or call 407-560-PASS

49   Move to Florida!

i   *You Can Save: Up to 45% at a Walt Disney World Resort*

ii   Well, OK, maybe you don't have to actually move here, but do you live in Florida now? If so, you are entitled to some great discounted and special tickets from Disney as well! Being a Walt Disney World Resort Passholder is a great value and includes some special benefits, but Florida residents can enjoy even **more** savings (and options)!

iii   **Annual Pass Discounts** — Florida residents get big discounts on Annual Passes and Premium Annual Passes, as well as Seasonal Passes (see below).

iv   **Interest-Free Financing** — You can spread the cost of select Theme Park Annual Passes over 12 monthly payments with Disney's interest-free monthly payment program (which is available only to Florida residents).

v   **Florida Resident Seasonal Pass** — The Florida Resident Seasonal Pass is a specially-priced Annual Pass that gives admission to all four of the major Walt Disney World theme parks, with blackout dates during the busiest times of year. Seasonal Passholders receive the same discounts on resort rooms, meals and merchandise as regular Annual Passholders. However, the Seasonal Pass does NOT include free parking.

vi   **Magic Your Way Ticket Discounts** — Florida Residents can save on a variety of ticket options, ranging from single day passes to Florida Resident 4-Day Tickets (Blackout dates apply and Florida Resident 3-Day and 4-Day Tickets expire 6 months after first use.)

vii   **Florida Resident Weekday Select Pass** — Florida residents can enjoy all 4 Disney theme parks Mondays through Fridays only during select times of the year. This exclusive Florida Resident pass is Disney's lowest-priced option. While the special Passholder discounts on Resort Hotels, dining, merchandise and more still apply, there are a number of blackout dates throughout the year.

viii   **Florida Resident Epcot After 4 p.m. Annual Pass** — Locals can enjoy Epcot after 4:00pm, with this ticket option. This is perfect for dining in World Showcase, hitting some of your favorite attractions, watching *"IllumiNations: Reflections of Earth"* or just wandering the World Showcase promenade.

This pass also includes special Passholder discounts on Resort Hotels, dining, merchandise, and exclusive Passholder special events and privileges.

ix **Florida Resident Water Parks After 2 p.m. Annual Pass** — Live in Florida and want to hit Blizzard Beach or Typhoon Lagoon with your family? This pass entitles you to unlimited visits to the water parks with admission only after 2:00pm (A Water Park Annual Pass or single-day ticket is available as well, but is not eligible under the Monthly Payment program)

x **Other Discounted Tickets For Florida Residents** — Occasionally Disney will release unexpected discounts for a specified period of time. *For example, in 2012, Disney offered Florida residents a discounted 3 or 4-day "Wild For Disney" pass for $99 and $129 plus tax, respectively.* Be sure to monitor the Florida resident page of Disney.com to see new offers!

xi **Disney Resort Hotel Discounts** —

a. Florida Residents enjoy great rates at Disney Resort hotels! Save when you stay in the middle of the magic — and enjoy all the benefits and conveniences of Disney accommodations.

b. Discounts can be as much as 45% off "rack" (normal advertised) rates often times around 30–35%. Sometimes, they also have special tickets and promotions for Florida residents who don't have an Annual or Seasonal Pass.

xii **But there's just one thing** — You actually have to live IN Florida (not just want to live here, own a vacation home or timeshare, etc.) in order to take advantage of Disney's Florida Resident discounts. In order to qualify for Florida Resident pass discounts, you have to show proof of residency such as a valid Florida driver's license or Florida state ID card, showing a Florida address

You can learn more about saving money on Disney ticket options by listening to WDW Radio Show #37!

102
WAYS
TO SAVE MONEY
FOR AND AT
WALT DISNEY WORLD

BY LOU MONGELLO

DISNEY RESORTS

WHERE TO STAY

50 **Stay at a Walt Disney World Resort — Think you can't afford it? Think again!**

i   Disney makes it easy for visitors on any budget to be a part of the magic and stay at a Walt Disney World Resort hotel. Not only can you afford it, but you also can actually SAVE money by staying on property. Click here to view all Resorts and Rates at http://DisneyWorld.com.

ii   Disney categorizes its resort hotels as VALUE, MODERATE, DELUXE, and HOME AWAY FROM HOME (DVC). Depending upon your budget and the promotions available, different resort types may be within your budget. All provide the legendary Disney service; the cost varies according to the size of accommodations and variety of amenities available.

iii   **Value Resorts:** The value resort is generally the most affordable Disney hotel category and is favored by the budget-conscious. If you are looking for the most affordable resort property, without missing the legendary Disney service, the value resort is for you! There are FIVE value resorts on Disney property. That means that there are nearly 10,000 (8,640 standard rooms in the Value category) starting as low as $82 per night.

   a.   *You Can Save: Around $200 per night by staying at a Value Resort over a Deluxe Resort*

b.   Disney's All-Star Movies Resort — Located near Disney's Animal Kingdom, this resort has 1,920 rooms and features giant icons and theming that salute classic Disney films.

c.   Disney's All-Star Music Resort — Located near Disney's Animal Kingdom, this 1,604-room hotel also has 214 family suites and celebrates the love of music.

d.   Disney's All-Star Sports Resort — Located near Disney's Animal Kingdom, Disney's All-Star Sports Resort celebrates the fun of all types of sports in a 1,920-room hotel.

e.   Disney's Pop Century Resort — Located near the ESPN Wide World of Sports complex, Disney's Pop Century Resort has 2,880 rooms featuring giant icons saluting 20th-century pop culture.

f.   Disney's Art of Animation Resort — Located near the ESPN Wide World of Sports complex, Disney's newest resort invites you to become a part of your favorite animated films such as Finding Nemo, Cars, The Lion King and The Little Mermaid in both the 1,120 family suites and 864 standard rooms *(in The Little Mermaid section)*. Note that the additional 1,078 family suites are priced higher than a standard, but are also located within the Value Resorts. Most will accommodate a party of up to six guests. Learn more about this exciting new Disney resort by listening to WDW Radio Show #272: Art of Animation Review

iv   **When to Consider a More Expensive Hotel Category**

a. **Party Size** — Depending upon your party size, a more expensive resort category MAY be more affordable option. For example, value resort rooms allow for only four guests over the age of three in a room (excluding family suites.) If you are a party of five, a moderate category room at Port Orleans-Riverside may be more affordable than two value bedrooms or a family suite. Authorized Disney Vacation planners can help you understand your options and determine the most economical choice for your family. See here for Disney's advice for families of five or more.

b. **Available Disney Promotion** — Certain Disney promotions (such as free dining) are extremely popular and book very quickly. You might discover there are no rooms available at a value resort during this time, but a moderate could still be within your budget when you factor in the money you will save with the free dining promotion. Know your budget and don't be afraid to play with options on the Walt Disney World website.

c. **Park v. Resort Time** — If your family vacation style is to relax in the room, play at the pool, and spend a couple hours in a park, you may want to consider a moderate or deluxe resort. These have larger accommodations that suit the more laid-back style. Value resorts use space efficiently, and if you plan to be staying in the hotel for a good part of each vacation day, your vacation experience may be worth the higher-priced resort category.

v **Other Ways You Save by Staying in a Disney Resort Hotel:**

a. **Disney Transportation** is free for Disney resort guests. Whether you use the Disney monorail, bus or boat system.... it's all free!

b. Magical Express a free bus service that runs between the Orlando airport and the onsite hotels, saves you the expense of a taxi or a rental car. Have questions about Disney's Magical Express? Check out WDW Radio Show #167, where I review the process of using Magical Express!

c. **If You Have A Car**: Parking at the theme parks is free for Walt Disney World resort guests. Be sure your parking pass is on the dashboard and clearly visible when you arrive at the parks.

d. **Benefits In The Parks**

- Extra Magic Hours

  - "Extra magic hours" allow you to enter one park each day either an hour before offsite guests or to remain in that park after it's officially closed to offsite guests! Note that Disney announces in advance which parks have these hours on specific dates and times. When checking in, be sure to ask for an Extra Magic Hours schedule.

  - Extra Magic hours give you access to the parks with fewer guests, allowing you to maximize your time. And remember: time is money!

- Package Pick Up This service allows you to have anything you buy in the parks delivered to your resort hotel! You can purchase those awesome souvenirs (that you purchased with all the money you have saved) and have them delivered to your Walt Disney World Resort hotel. This saves your back from carrying these items all around and also saves you time—you don't have to run around to souvenir shops at the end of a long day. Shop in the morning, when the shops are less crowded, and your treasures will be awaiting your return!

e. **Benefits Around The Resort**

- Charging privileges. Your Walt Disney World room key also serves as your theme park ticket AND as a credit card that allows you to charge anything you spend in Disney World. All your purchases — restaurants, souvenirs shops, snacks — can be placed on this card, and they are then centralized on your resort account.

- Note that the charging privileges can be turned off on your children's room keys, to avoid potential problems if the key is lost.

- You can book easy, affordable packages that already include food plans and discounted tickets! (See detailed discussion of the Disney Dining Plan and how it can save you up to 40% on your dining expenses in Dining Section)

- The Bottom line: Staying at a Walt Disney World Resort Hotel saves money, while extending the Disney experience

51 **Stay in the Family Suites** — Walt Disney World offers family suite options at both the Art of Animation and All Star Music Resorts.

i   Family suites are a great choice if your travel party consists of five or six members. This option saves you having to reserve two rooms at a value resort and splitting your party.

ii   Family suites are also an excellent consideration if your travel style involves relaxing by the pool, watching a family movie, or taking afternoon naps. The family suite offers the extra space to a family that will be spending more than just sleeping hours in their room.

iii   Because they offer a mini kitchen, family suites offer the ability to save on dining expenses, as food can be purchased, stored, and prepared in the room.

iv   Family suites include: Queen-size bed, double-size sleeper sofa, 1 convertible sleeper chair, and 1 convertible sleeper ottoman, living room, 2 bathrooms, vanity area with sink, mini-kitchen with microwave, table and chairs, and in-room wall safe

DID YOU KNOW? Fort Wilderness used to have its own railroad! *The Wilderness Line Railway* ran from 1974–1979, offering guests a unique mode of transportation through the large campground.

52   Go Camping... at Walt Disney World

i   *"Ain't nuthin' like the great outdoors..."* sing the musical bears of the Country Bear Jamboree in Frontierland in Walt Disney World, and they're right!

ii Walt Disney World's Fort Wilderness is a family-friendly way to connect with nature without having to "rough it."

    a. Got a tent or an RV? Families who are avid campers can save a significant amount off the cost of a resort hotel room by bringing their Recreational Vehicle or tent to Disney's Fort Wilderness.

        • Fort Wilderness campsites come equipped with "privacy-enhancing" landscaping, water, cable television and electrical hook-ups. Also included are a picnic table and a charcoal grill. Most sites also include a sewer hook-up, and some even permit pets!

    b. You can cut your hotel bill to under $60 per night by staying at the Fort Wilderness Resort & Campground at one of their beautiful pop-up campsites.

    c. You still maintain many of the amenities of a Disney Resort when staying at Fort Wilderness. Options for inexpensive fun include two heated outdoor pools, tennis, horseshoes, shuffleboard, fishing, bicycling, pony rides and horseback trail riding, and nightly wagon rides around the resort.

    d. A great activity here includes the traditional nightly campfire sing-a-long and marshmallow roast with Chip 'n Dale, followed by a G-rated Disney double feature on a huge outdoor screen under the stars.

    e. Transportation to the parks is still included, with buses stopping at many bus stops throughout the sprawling campground. There also is a boat launch that takes you directly to the Magic Kingdom.

f. Save even more while staying at Fort Wilderness by bringing your own food and preparing meals within the comfort of your RV.

53 Invest in Concierge Level Rooms or Deluxe Villas —

i Concierge (or "Club-Level") rooms can sometimes be obtained at a discount. Concierge level rooms can be found at Disney's Polynesian Resort, Disney's Grand Floridian Resort and Spa, Disney's Contemporary Resort, Disney's Wilderness Lodge, Disney's Yacht Club Resort, Disney's Beach Club Resort, Disney's Animal Kingdom Lodge, Disney's Boardwalk Inn, and Disney's Coronado Springs Resort. The Deluxe Villas at the Disney Vacation Club resorts (Disney's Old Key West Resort, Disney's Boardwalk Villas, Disney's Beach Club Villas, Disney's Villas at Wilderness Lodge, Disney's Saratoga Springs Resort & Spa, Disney's Animal Kingdom Villas and Disney's Bay Lake Tower Resort) are discounted at times. Discounts are most common at Old Key West and Saratoga Springs resorts.

ii While concierge options or deluxe resorts are more expensive than value or moderate resorts, they offer nice perks that can help you save money in other ways:

a. Concierge services: Concierge level guests have access to concierge planning services, which will assist with making reservations for dining and experiences.

b. Concierge guests also have exclusive access to a lounge that provides food and snacks throughout the day, including continental breakfasts, afternoon snacks, evening appetizers, and nighttime desserts.

iii   Deluxe Villas have full kitchens and laundry facilities. If you enjoy cooking or want to have a more relaxed vacation style, you can purchase food at a local grocery store and prepare your meals in your villa. You also can get all that laundry done, enabling you to pack less and save on the cost of the resort laundry facilities.

54 **Cut Out That View!** Another simple way to save money (and use it elsewhere on your vacation!) is by NOT splurging on certain things — like your room view. Disney offers a variety of rooms views, from standard to preferred, garden, pool (standard and preferred), water, and savannah (at Disney's Animal Kingdom Lodge).

i   *You Can Save: $15.00–150.00 Per Night*

ii   If you're looking for a way to save at Walt Disney World, not getting a "preferred view" room is one easy way. Simply put, Preferred Rooms may have everything from a water, lagoon, theme park or savannah view, while a regular room may overlook trees, a parking lot, another part of the resort, etc. Disney charges a premium for views that are considered preferable.

iii   But you have to ask yourself — how much time am I spending in my room? Will we be going "commando" style from dawn until the park closes? If so, and the view isn't important to you (or you'll never see it), this is an easy way to save.

DID YOU KNOW? The Shades of Green Resort used to be called The Golf Resort, and then the Disney Inn. On February 1, 1994, the Department of Defense (DOD) leased the Disney Inn for exclusive use by retired and active duty military personnel and their families. The DOD subsequently purchased the resort and renamed it "Shades of Green" to signify the camoflauge uniforms worn by the armed forces.

55 Disney Honors The Military and Their Families

i   Disney continues its tradition of honoring armed forces servicemen and women with specially discounted tickets. There also is an entire resort specifically for the members of the armed services and their families.

ii   Shades of Green® at Walt Disney World is a 27 acre Armed Forces Recreation Center (AFRC) located just a hop, skip, and a jump away from the Magic Kingdom and near two PGA Championship golf courses. Shades of Green is operated by the U.S. Army, and has 583 rooms that can sleep up to five people as well as a limited number of family suites.

   a.   *You Can Save: Discounts are based on rank, but can be significant, possibly up to 50% off a comparable Walt Disney World Resort*

   b.   The rooms and the hallways are spacious and include complimentary Wi-Fi to all guests.

   c.   Shades of Green buses provide complimentary transportation to any of the Disney attractions, and guests can participate in the Extra Magic Hours program as well.

d. There are two restaurants at the resort, Mangino's and Garden Gallery, where kids, up to the age of 6, eat FREE. There are also two swimming pools and a modern fitness center.

iii Other Walt Disney World Resort Military Discounts

a. *You Can Save: Up to 30% off at a Value Resort*

b. During certain times of year, Disney offers active duty and retired members of the armed services discounts that can be up to 30% off of a Value Resort, 35% off of a Moderate Resort or Cabin at Ft. Wilderness Campground and 40% off of a Deluxe Resort or a Deluxe Villa Resort. Inquire about available discounts when booking or ask your Authorized Disney Vacation Planner

56 Stay At a Nearby Hotel

ii But wait! You just told me to stay ON Walt Disney World property, right? True. But if you're on a really tight budget, you can stay close to the Walt Disney World Resort in a nearby hotel or motel, with rates that are lower than a resort on Walt Disney World property. You WILL lose out on all of the amenities, benefits, theming, freebies and much more, but if every penny counts, it may be something to consider. Checking sites like Priceline.com, Expedia.com and Orbitz.com will give you the best options, as well as photos and reader reviews.

a. A great alternative to a Disney Resort Hotel include the Swan and Dolphin Hotels. Located on Disney property, right behind Epcot and across the street from Disney's Hollywood Studios, these beautiful accommodations are run by Westin properties.

b. Guests at the Swan and Dolphin are eligible to use Disney transportation, can take advantage of Extra Magic Hours, and have free parking privileges in the theme parks.

c. The Swan and Dolphin often offer special promotions, different from the Walt Disney resort hotels. For example, for the year 2013, there are special discounts for teachers and educational support staff at these properties (proof of employment is required at check in.)

d. Note that if you drive a car to the Swan and Dolphin, they do charge a parking fee ($15 a day for self-parking and $23 for valet.)

e. For more on special packages and discounts at the Swan and Dolphin, check this link.

f. You can also learn more by listening to WDW Radio Show #225

57 Get a House

i *You Can Save: Thousands on Hotels and Dining!*

ii I don't mean to BUY a house (although you'll see the benefits of being a Florida Resident in Tip #49), but if you are vacationing with a large or extended family, renting a vacation home is a great option that will also afford you big savings

iii Vacation home rentals not only will let you save a great deal in the cost of your hotel room(s), but they are an overall great vacation value with many other advantages as well:

a. Less expensive per night than a single hotel room.

b. A large family, multiple families or groups can rent a house for sometimes half of what two hotel rooms could cost. Some vacation homes can accommodate as many as 40 people! Even the least expensive rooms at Disney have a four person limit, meaning a large, extended family could need 10 rooms at a value resort, versus one vacation home.

c. Having a full kitchen allows you to save hundreds by cooking meals at the home instead of eating out for three meals per day.

d. As each home has a free washer and dryer, you can pack less (carrying less luggage will save you on airline fees) and have room to bring back souvenirs you bought with the money you saved!

e. Instead of a 300 sq. ft. room with bathroom, a vacation home gives you much more space to spread out and enjoy, including a living room, full kitchen, dining room, multiple master bedrooms, patio and (if you choose) a private pool. Instead of 300 sq feet, you can get 2,000 sq feet — even more room than one of Disney's deluxe resorts.

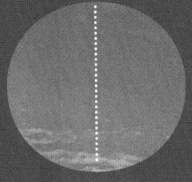

102
WAYS
TO SAVE MONEY
FOR AND AT
WALT DISNEY WORLD

BY LOU MONGELLO

TO BOOK A PACKAGE...
OR NOT

58 Book a Room-Only Rate

i   Often times, the best deal on a Walt Disney World resort hotel is by booking a room-only rate (which means only the hotel, with no tickets, dining packages, etc.) — especially if you utilize some of the discounts I discuss in this guide.

ii Room-only reservations also normally provide for more flexible cancellation policies, as well as different payment dates, than a package booked through the Walt Disney Travel Company directly.

    a.   For example, you normally only need to pay one night's room rate as a deposit when reserving your room, with final payment due at check-in.

    b.   You can also cancel or change your reservation with no penalties up until 5 days prior to check-in.

iii When booking a travel package, you normally need to pay a $200 deposit, with final payment due within 45 days of your check-in date. Be sure and check with your travel agent, provider or the Walt Disney Travel Company for all terms and payment requirements.

59 Know When to Book a Package

i   On the other side of the coin, booking a package may be a good deal for you and your family! In some cases, a package that includes your room, park tickets, dining (see Dining Section) and even airfare may be a better option, saving you both money AND time.

ii Remember that time IS money, and having to check multiple rates from a variety of sources, comparing deals, making reservations, etc. are all fun, but time-consuming and sometimes a bit frustrating as you juggle to get the best deal possible. Sometimes, paying for the convenience is certainly worth it when you factor your "sweat equity" into the equation. Plus, you never know what kind of deal on a vacation package you may find by calling your travel agent, the Walt Disney Travel Company or by looking at DisneyWorld.com

60 **Use Those Discount Codes** — Just like many online retailers, Disney often offers discount codes and special offers on resort rooms and Magic Your Way vacation packages. Knowing where to find them is the important part!

i *You Can Save: Up to 40% Off Your Resort Room*

ii **Special Offers** — The easiest way to find Disney's current discounts is by visiting that section of their web site. It may not be right in the middle of the home page, but look in the drop-down menus or go right to http://disneyworld.disney.go.com/special-offers/ to find current available offers on everything from rooms to tickets, to golf and recreation and more!

iii **Pin Codes and Discount Codes:**

    a. *You Can Save: Up to 40% at a Deluxe Resort*

    b. **Pin Codes** — I always suggest to Walt Disney World visitors that they stay on property, take every survey that's offered (whether online or by a survey taker at the park entrances), and sign up for any email lists directly from Disney. Also, be sure and visit DisneyWorld.com and create an account on the site. Why? Throughout the year, Disney often emails special invitations and "Pin Codes" to guests who have stayed at a Walt Disney World Resort in the past. The codes vary throughout the year, and offer discounts that may include everything from free dining to discounted room rates of up to 40% off! These codes are specifically generated for YOU, and are NOT meant to be shared with friends, family or on Facebook and Twitter!

c. **Discount Codes** — If Disney offers a special discount, they normally assign a special code to it, called a "Discount Code" (thank you, Captain Obvious). For example, if you are a Disney Visa cardholder, you may be offered a special discount code for free dining, while there may be a separate code for the same discount available to the general public. How you get it doesn't matter — just be on the lookout! But here's the best part: you often don't even need to know the code at all! When booking through your travel agent or directly with the Walt Disney Travel Company, ask about any discounts, and let them know about being a cardholder, Annual Passholder, etc. They will search for and apply any discount codes that may be available. Discounts aren't always available, or might not fit into the exact time, resort or plan you had in mind, but if and when they work, they can save you hundreds of dollars on your next vacation!

102
WAYS
TO SAVE MONEY
FOR AND AT
WALT DISNEY WORLD

BY LOU MONGELLO

DINING

THINK ABOUT WHERE (AND HOW) YOU WANT TO EAT... *BEFORE* YOU GO ON VACATION (No, really!)

61 **Make Advanced Dining Reservations (ADR's)** — Saving time by planning where you are going to eat equates to saving money — your time is valuable at Walt Disney World, so if you have a plan and reservations, you'll spend less time waiting and more time having fun — thus, more value for your dollar!

i   Many Disney table-service restaurants are quite popular and book quickly. You can make dining reservations up to 180 days in advance by calling (407) WDW-DINE or online at Disney Dining. Guests under 18 years of age must have a parent or guardian's permission to call.

ii   **Word to the Wise:** Carefully track the dining reservations you make, as missed reservations result in a $10 penalty charged to the credit card you used to hold the reservation. I suggest you make a card of your ADR locations, dates, times, and confirmation numbers and keep with your wallet so you can access that information easily. Alternatively, keep the information in a file on your smart phone, with 407-WDW-DINE on "speed dial." Alternatively, download the "My Disney Experience" app to your smartphone, and link your reservations there, so you always have easy access to your dining locations and times. (Download the free app here)"

62   Add the Disney Dining Plan to your package reservation

i   *You Can Save: Up to 30% on Your Meals*

ii   The "Disney Dining Plan" is an option available exclusively to Guests of select Walt Disney World Resort hotels who book a Magic Your Way Vacation Package or use Disney Vacation Club (DVC) points. It can be a great money-saving add-on... and can also be quite confusing.

iii   With the Disney Dining Plan, you are basically pre-purchasing a specific number of dining credits. For each night of your stay, everyone on your reservation gets a specific number of "vouchers" for quick service meals, table service meals, and snacks. The type of plan you choose determines how many credits of each type of meal you will receive per day.

iv   As of 2013, there were five different versions of the dining plan: Quick Service Dining Plan, Dining Plan, Deluxe Dining Plan, Premium Dining Plan, and Platinum Dining Plan.

Note that children under the age of three are not eligible to participate in any of the Disney Dining Plan.

a. **Quick Service Dining Plan** — Guests receive: Two Quick-Service Meal credits and one snack credit per person, per night of the package, as well as one refillable mug per person valid for the length of the package.

b. **Standard/Regular Dining Plan** — Guests receive: One Quick-Service Meal, one snack and one Table-Service Meal per person, per night of the package stay for everyone in the party ages 3 and over, as well as one Resort refillable drink mug per person, that is valid for the length of your stay.

c. **Deluxe Disney Dining Plan** — Guests receive: Three meal credits (which can be used at a counter service or table service restaurant) and two snack credits per person, per night of the package, as well as one refillable mug per person in the package good for use during the length of the package.

d. **Premium Dining Plan** — Guests receive: Three meal credits (which can be used at a counter service or table service restaurant) and two snack credits per person, per night of your package, as well as one refillable mug per person in the package good for use during the length of the package. Additionally, guests on the Premium Dining Plan receive: unlimited selected recreation, including golf, golf lessons, miniature golf, guided fishing excursions, parasailing, water skiing, wake boarding, watercraft rentals, bike rentals, cane pole fishing, tennis, horseback trail rides, pony ride, horse-drawn carriage rides, and archery.

e. **Platinum Dining Plan** — Guests receive: Three meal credits (which can be used at a counter service or table service restaurant) and two snack credits per person, per night of your package, as well as one refillable mug per person in the package good for use during the length of the package. Additionally, guests on the Platinum Dining Plan receive:

- Unlimited selected recreation, including golf, golf lessons, miniature golf, guided fishing excursions, parasailing, water skiing, wake boarding, watercraft rentals, bike rentals, cane pole fishing, tennis, horseback trail rides, pony ride, horse-drawn carriage rides, and archery.

- Unlimited admission to select theme park tours

- Cirque du Soleil *La Nouba* ticket for each person

- Admission to the children's activity centers.

- Spa treatments

- PhotoPass products

- Richard Petty Ride-Along Experience, and more — *See package details for specific information.*

v   You don't get a physical "voucher," but your Key to the World card (which is your room key) keeps track of how many meals you have used and have remaining. After your meal, your printed receipt will show you the number of credits remaining, and you can always ask your server or Guest Services at your resort to confirm your number of remaining credits.

a. You can use your credits any way you want — two counter services one day, three snacks and a table service the next — there is no required order for their use. If you don't use all of your credits, they expire on midnight of the night you check out. They are not redeemable for cash or future visits.

b. **Bonus Tip:** Remember that you can also use your snack credits to bring home some "edible souvenirs" for yourself or your family/friends such as candy, lollipops, crisped rice treats, fudge, Chip and Dale snack bags and Tiny Treats.

vi The details and intricacies of the Dining Plans can be an entire section of this Guide itself, and the details of the Plans may change from time to time, but there are some important guidelines when considering if the plan is right for you and your family:

a. You must purchase the plan for your entire stay and for each person staying in your hotel room.

b. The Dining Plan option is not available to those booking "room only" reservations or Florida resident room-only discounts.

c. The Disney Dining Plan prices range from around $35 per adult per night and $12 per child under the age of 10 per night for the Quick Service Dining Plan to $90 per adult per night and $12 per child under the age of 10 per night for the Deluxe Plan.

d. Adult alcoholic beverages are not included on the dining plan. Gratuities are not included unless otherwise indicated.

e. An automatic 18% gratuity charge will be added to your bill for parties of 6 or more.

f. The Disney Dining Plan can NOT be added on to your reservation once you have arrived at your resort. It must be added to your reservation prior to arriving at Walt Disney World, usually at least 48 hours in advance.

g. Although the plans cannot be used for children under the age of 3, toddlers can share your meal at counter service and table service restaurants, or you will need to purchase or bring food for your little one. Remember, though, that children under the age of 3 do not need a theme park ticket, so there is considerable savings there.

h. Some of Disney's dining experiences are known as "Signature Dining" restaurants, and require 2 table service dining plan credits per person per meal. These locations are normally a bit more upscale, special or popular and include (but may not be limited to) Cinderella's Royal Table, Jiko, Flying Fish Cafe, California Grill, Citricos, Narcoosee's, Artist Point, Yachtsman Steakhouse, LeCellier Steakhouse, Bistro de Paris, Monsieur Paul, Hollywood Brown Derby, Fulton's Crab House, and Wolfgang Puck Dining Room. Guests on the Premium and Platinum plans have no distinction between one and two credit meals.

i. A table service meal may be used for one Character Dining Experience (except Cinderella's Royal Table, which will require 2 table service meals).

j. Two table service meals may be exchanged for one of the following:

- One Signature Dining Experience, including appetizer (guests 3–9 ONLY), entrée, dessert, plus non-alcoholic beverage

- One Disney Dinner Show (Category 2 or 3 seating at either show, or Category 1 seating at the 9:30 pm Hoop-Dee-Doo Musical Revue)

- One room service meal, including appetizer (lunch & dinner, guests 3–9 ONLY), entrée, dessert (lunch and dinner), plus non-alcoholic beverage

- One Pizza Delivery — 1 pizza, 2 single-serving, non-alcoholic beverages, 2 desserts

k. If you use all of your dining credits, the Disney Dining Plan can save you 20–40% on your meals at Walt Disney World.

l. Is the Dining Plan right for you? When trying to decide if you should invest in the dining plan (or WHICH dining plan to invest in), there are some questions you should ask yourself and discuss as a family:

- How do you and your family (especially the kids) eat? Are there picky eaters who will only want burgers and hot dogs? The answers to these questions can affect the types and number of restaurants on your list.

- What time of day do you usually eat your big meal? If you traditionally have a large lunch and light dinner, this may affect which plan you want — and the number of credits you need.

- How much time do you want to spend while dining? Often a table service meal can take upwards of two hours (this can vary a great deal), which clearly has an effect on your time with the rides!

- How much do you traditionally eat in a day? The dining plan can be a lot of food for a family. If you have multiple table service meals in one day, dining can start to feel like a chore. (What? Did I say that?)

- What are your resort accommodations like? If you have a full kitchen, you may want to be eating breakfast and/or dinner in the room, which would reduce the need for a dining plan.

m. Used properly, the dining plan can save you substantial money. However, you MUST be willing to do your homework, plan (make reservations!) ahead, adjust your schedule around those reservation times, and keep track of your dining — and snack credit — allotments. Otherwise, you are potentially wasting your investment.

vii Visit DisneyWorld.com or contact an Authorized Disney Vacation Planner for more details or if you have any questions, as there are MANY options, including a Quick-Service Dining Plan, Deluxe Dining Plan, Platinum Dining Plan and more.

viii **Bonus Tip: Lou's Top Ten Favorite Snack Credit Treats!**

a. **Magic Kingdom**

- Pineapple Dole Whip — Aloha Isle in Adventureland

- Mickey Pretzel — Frontierland Churro/Pretzel Cart

- Chili-Cheese Fries — Pecos Bill's Tall Tale Inn & Café in Frontierland

- To learn more about the snack credits available in the New Fantasyland, check out this fun video at WDWRadio.com, Big Top Souvenirs and Treats at Storybook Circus. We also have a video feature on the Best Magic Kingdom Snacks for Under $5

b. **Epcot**

- School Bread — Kringla Bakeri Og Kafe in Norway

- Dark Chocolate Caramel with Sea Salt — Karamel Kuche in Germany

- Check out WDW Radio Show #209 for fun descriptions and more information about EPCOT snacks!

- Want to try some international teas? Check out this video!

c. **Disney's Hollywood Studios**

- Carrot Cake Cookie — Writer's Stop

- Nachos with Cheese — Herbie's Drive-In (located near Lights, Motor, Action! Stunt Show)

- Funnel Cake — Oasis Canteen at Echo Lake

- Want to find out the BEST snack in Disney's Hollywood Studios? Check out my quest to find the answer!

d. **Disney's Animal Kingdom**

- Chicken Fried Rice — Yak & Yeti Local Foods Café in Asia

- Jalapeno Cheese Stuffed Pretzel — Safari Pretzel on Discovery Island

63 Plan to Travel during Free Dining Time in Walt Disney World

ii Wait... WHAT? FREE dining? Come on... what's the catch? Believe it or not, you CAN get the Disney Dining Plan for FREE. No catches, no tricks, no secret codes! Over the past few years, Disney has been offering special promotions at select times of year, which allows guests booking Walt Disney World Resort hotel stays receive the Dining Plan for free as part of their vacation package. The dates and offers have varied, but generally speaking, if you book a qualifying vacation package at a moderate or deluxe resort, you will receive the Standard Dining Plan (which includes 1 counter-service meal credit, 1 table-service meal credit, and 1 snack credit per person, per night of stay) at no additional cost. While you have the option of upgrading to a Deluxe plan for an additional cost, the savings of the free dining plan work out to about $100+ per night savings for a family of four.

a. For example, if Disney offers a free Disney Dining Plan when you purchase a non-discounted 6-night/7-day Magic Your Way room and ticket package at select Disney Moderate Resorts, you may get a rate of somewhere around $86 per person, per day for a family of 4 in a standard room for a total package price of $2,421. That's would be a savings of more than $1,000!

b. Note that because the packages normally include a room at the full "rack rate," you may be able to work out a better deal for yourself by finding a resort room at a lower price and paying for your food (using this Guide's Dining tips will help!)

iii **Want to see if Free Dining is available during your travel dates?** Visit DisneyWorld.com or your Authorized Disney Vacation Planner. I use and recommend MouseFanTravel.com.

64 Purchase a Tables in Wonderland Membership

i *You Can Save: 20% on (almost) Every Meal & More!*

ii If you are an Annual Passholder, you are entitled to purchase a "Tables in Wonderland" discount dining card. Formerly known as the "Disney Dining Experience," Tables in Wonderland offers Florida Residents, Disney Vacation Club members, and Annual Passholders 20% off of all food and beverage purchases (including alcohol) at the participating Disney restaurants. Be aware that your check will have an 18% gratuity added regardless of party size.

iii This membership program currently costs $125 for Florida Residents and $100 for Annual / Seasonal Passholders and

Disney Vacation Club Members. You can also add a second membership for your spouse or partner for only $50 more! There is also a fee for a lost or replacement cards.

iv   A "Tables in Wonderland" card can be purchased at any Disney Guest Services location by an Annual Passholder and/or Florida Resident age 21 or older.

v   "Tables in Wonderland" membership is good for 1 year from date of purchase. "Tables in Wonderland" does not offer renewals. Each time you purchase "Tables in Wonderland," it is just like purchasing a new membership.

vi   Note that one "Tables in Wonderland" can cover an entire family or group up to 10 people.

vii   Using the card just a few times will more than make up for the membership fee! "Tables in Wonderland" can give guests a HUGE savings in the cost of food — and more! How?

a.   **Groups** — The "Tables in Wonderland" discount is good for up to 10 people, as long as everyone is on the same check, and the Tables in Wonderland member is paying the bill (no splitting of checks allowed with the discount).

b.   If you have the "Tables in Wonderland" card, and your spouse has the "Tables in Wonderland" secondary card, together you may cover up to 20 people. Note that both members must live at the same address and be 21 years of age or older.

- **Valet Parking** — If you are dining at a Walt Disney World Resort that offers valet parking and are using your "Tables in Wonderland" card, they will waive the valet parking fee — let the attendant know and be sure to have your card and restaurant receipt when you pick up your vehicle.

c. **Theme Park Parking** — Theme Park parking is complimentary to members, for the sole purpose of dining. Before 5:00pm, you still pay for parking at the Toll Plaza. Visit Guest Relations on your way out of the Theme Park, and if it has been less than 3 hours, show your membership card and dining receipt for reimbursement for parking. After 5:00 p.m., members can show their membership card at the toll plaza to enter the parking lot at no cost.

- *You Can Save: $14 Per Day Per Vehicle to Park*

d. **Special Events** — "Tables in Wonderland" also send their members special invitations to member-only events, such as exclusive Food and Wine Festival events, wine tasting dinners, celebrity chef dinners, and much more.

viii Also note that the "Tables in Wonderland" discount is not available on holidays including New Year's Eve, Year Year's Day, Easter, Mother's Day, Fourth of July, Thanksgiving, Christmas Eve and Christmas Day. Starting in 2014, additional blackout dates will be in effect for specific restaurants. As always, be sure to investigate all the details before purchasing to make sure this program is the best investment for your travel needs.

ix For more information, you can call "Tables in Wonderland" at 407-566-5858 or visit TablesInWonderland.com

65 Become an Annual Passholder

i Remember a few pages back where I recommended becoming a Walt Disney World Annual Passholder? Here's another reason why!

ii Disney offers additional dining benefits and discounts to Annual Passholders, including:

a. A variety of dining discounts at Walt Disney World Resort Theme Parks. For example, at Epcot, you can save 10% on regularly priced food and non-alcoholic beverages Monday through Friday during lunch hours at participating Epcot Table-Service locations like China's Nine Dragons Restaurant®, Japan's Teppan Edo and Tokyo Dining, Tutto Italia Ristorante in Italy, Restaurant

Marrakesh® in Morocco and the San Angel Inn® restaurant in Mexico. Note that certain holiday blackout dates apply. At Hollywood & Vine at Disney's Hollywood Studios, Passholders save 10% on regularly priced food and non-alcoholic beverages at breakfast. Similar benefits exist at Disney's Animal Kingdom restaurants.

b. At Downtown Disney, Annual Passholder savings can be even more, with 10% off any purchase at Ghirardelli® Soda Fountain & Chocolate Shop, discounts up to 20% off your meal at Fulton's Crab House, 20% off food and non-alcoholic beverages daily in the House of Blues® prior to 4:00 p.m. and 10% off after 4:00 p.m. for the Passholder and up to 5 Guests. Rainforest Café®, T-Rex Café® and many others also offer dining discounts starting at 10% off. Reserve online or by calling (407) WDW-DINE or (407) 939-3463 , unless otherwise noted.

c. Also visit http://disneyworld.disney.go.com/passholder-program/dining-discounts/ for the latest information

102
WAYS
TO SAVE MONEY
FOR AND AT
WALT DISNEY WORLD

BY LOU MONGELLO

WHAT TO PACK... OR SHIP

When packing for a Walt Disney World vacation, there is SO much you'll need and want to bring. Clothes, shoes, toiletries, kids' toys, gadgets and gizmos aplenty... the list goes on and on (and on). With airlines charging for second (and sometimes first) bags checked and additional fees for overweight suitcases , you need to be conscious of what you pack in your checked baggage. Plus, chances are you'll be coming home with more than you when you left (souvenirs!), so you'll need some additional space as well. So what's the best way to pack AND save money? SHIP and SHOP!

66 Ship it There

i   Did you know that Guests staying at Walt Disney World Resort hotels can have packages shipped to the resort and stored

prior to their check-in? This means that you can ship vacation necessities purchased at home to your resort, without taking up valuable (and expensive) space in your luggage. Many of the items you may want to have in your room or when you're in the parks can be shipped ahead of time.

ii   While it makes sense to keep important, valuable and necessary items close to you in a backpack or purse (such as any medicines and important documents), here are just a few things you can consider shipping ahead of time to save money:

a.   **Food:** Bottles of water, cereal, granola bars, peanut butter, Pop Tarts (I'm still a kid at heart), microwave popcorn, and other non-perishable snacks to eat in your room or take to the parks. Consider bringing a small filtered water pitcher and refillable bottles. You can have fresh clean water right from the tap, fill up your bottles and bring them into the parks in your backpack or bag!

   • If you are planning on sending down a lot of water or liquids like soda, alcohol, etc., you may want to look into a service like GardenGrocer.com, which will deliver to your resort your grocery order you place online ahead of time. (There is a minimum order of $40 and small delivery fee. They offer free delivery for orders over $200).

   • You must place your order a minimum of 36 hours in advance but 72 hours or more is recommended.

b.   **Toiletries:** Sunblock, your favorite shampoo and conditioner, body wash, aloe (you never know if you may get a little sunburned), curling iron, perfume, hand sanitizer, contact lens solution, mouthwash

c. **Clothes:** Depending on when you visit, Florida CAN actually get cool (make that COLD!) at night, so think about shipping sweatshirts, jackets, extra shoes (in case your favorite pair gets wet—think 4:00 rain storm), and beach towels

d. **Kids' Stuff:** Diapers, baby food, moist towels, kids toys, board games to play in the room or by the pool

e. **Other Items**: Power strip, extra batteries for your camera or toys/games, your Disney trading pin collection, laundry supplies, swimming goggles and other pool accessories.

iii **How to Pack and Ship:** Be sure to pack everything securely and safely in a well-sealed package and send it to your resort via UPS or FedEx (so that you can track the package). Also, make certain you send it far enough in advance of your arrival date so that it arrives a day or two before you check-in. Make sure to address the package using the full, proper address of the resort. I suggest addressing the package in this manner:

- Guest: *Your Name*

- Reservation Number *(optional)*

- c/o Disney's Resort Name *(e.g. Disney's Resort Club)*

- Arrival Date: *MM/DD/YYYY*

- Full address: *(e.g. 1800 Epcot Resorts Boulevard)*

- City, State, Zip: *(e.g. Lake Buena Vista, FL 32830)*

67   Shop When You Get There

i   While shipping many items to your resort can save you money, shopping when you get to Orlando may be another way to economize. If you have a rental car or are willing to take a taxi, you can visit local stores like Walgreens, Walmart and Target (all of which are within a few miles of the Walt Disney World resort) to buy some of the items you may need. I don't suggest shopping at some of the smaller grocery stores nearest the tourist areas, as the prices at the larger, chain stores will likely be better. These are great for some pool toys, sundries, diapers, heavy items like soda, water, alcohol, etc.

ii   When you DO shop for items like souvenirs at Walt Disney World, you can actually have them shipped home for you right from the store! If you flew to Orlando, you may want to consider having your souvenirs shipped home directly from the merchandise locations on property. You will pay for shipping, of course (starting around $8.95), but Disney will not charge you sales tax on your purchase. You'll need to do a little math to see if it's worthwhile for you, but often the amount you save in tax will offset the amount you pay in shipping.

68   Ship It Home

i   The only bad part of a Walt Disney World vacation is that it eventually has to end. And on that fateful day when you start packing for home, you look around your room and see bags and boxes of souvenirs, dirty laundry, and things you may have forgotten you purchased.

    a.   **Ship It, Don't Pack It!** — Shipping prices are reasonable and with the new airline restrictions, it may be a more economical choice to ship home rather than bring an extra suitcase to lug souvenirs. Don't have a box? That's OK! Go to your resort's front desk or merchandise location and ask them for a box to ship your items home. They'll not only help find you a box, but seal it as well. Ask about the cost of shipping for larger items.

b. Also make sure that you ship any delicate items that contain liquid if you'll be traveling home on an airplane. There have been reports of vacationers having to leave expensive snow globes with airport security because they tucked them in their carry-on bags.

ii When you're ready to ship it home, you have a few money-saving options as well:

a. **Front Desk** — You can take your pre-packed, pre-labeled packages to the Front Desk or Concierge desk of most Walt Disney World Resort hotels and the Cast Members there will put them into the outgoing shipping service for you.

b. **Business Centers** — There are a number of Business Centers at resorts throughout Walt Disney World, including Disney's Boardwalk Resort, Disney's Contemporary Resort, Disney's Coronado Springs Resort, Disney's Grand Floridian Resort & Spa, Disney's Yacht Club and the Walt Disney World Swan and Dolphin Hotels. Here, they can help you pack and ship items home via US Postal Service, FedEx or UPS.

c. **Off-Property** — Neither is within walking distance (especially if you have large packages to ship), but there is a mailing center and FedEx location not far from Walt Disney World

- FedEx Office is located near the Crossroads shopping center, not far from Downtown Disney. It is open 24 hours a day on weekdays and until midnight on weekends and is located at 12181 S. Apopka Vineland Road (SR 535) just north of the intersection of Palm Parkway. Their phone number is 407-465-0085.

- The World Mail Center is located at the Vista Center Shoppes, 8546 Palm Parkway, just off SR 535 near Downtown Disney. Their phone number is 407-778-5912.

102
WAYS
TO SAVE MONEY
FOR AND AT
WALT DISNEY WORLD
BY LOU MONGELLO

WHILE YOU'RE THERE

69 Invest in a Refillable Mug

i   Walt Disney Resort hotels introduced a new refillable mug program called "Rapid Fill" in Summer, 2013.

ii "Rapid Fill" mugs allow Disney Resort guests to buy (or receive as part of their Disney Dining Plan) a Resort mug which can be refilled for a certain period of time, which is determined at the time of purchase. These mugs have an RFID chip embedded in them which will deactivate the mug when the designated time is complete, and prevent further refills.l

iii When the purchased period expires, the mug will automatically "deactivate." The beverage fountains have an easy-to-read LCD display to indicate the number of remaining refill days. The mugs may be used at any resort hotel quick service fountain (regardless of where it was original purchased). Expired mugs can not be reused, so you will need to purchase a new mug for each resort stay. You do not need to be a resort guest to purchase a refillable mug.

70 Use Your Refrigerator

i   *You Can Save: $100.00–$200.00 Per Week*

ii If you stay in a Walt Disney World resort, each room is equipped with a small refrigerator at no extra cost. This can be one of your biggest money-saving allies. *As of 2012, all of the Value Resorts now have complimentary mini-fridges in their rooms as well!*

a. Use your refrigerator to keep milk, juice, water, and other "breakfast basics." Bring (or purchase) dry cereal and you have an easy, inexpensive, fast breakfast in your room before heading out to the parks. A $5 box of cereal and a $2 carton of milk can feed your family of 4 for much less than even a counter-service breakfast. You can even bring (or buy if you do a grocery store run) disposable bowls and plastic spoons so you can eat breakfast in your room or by the pool. And because time is money, you can also use the time you save on having "to go" for breakfast and get to the parks early and get more done.

b. If you like to come back to the room midday (as is recommended, especially if you have young kids and during the hot summer months), you can also fix everyone a light snack or lunch before dinner. If you have a car and bought groceries (or had them delivered — see above), you can purchase some lunch meat and bread and give everyone a full lunch for just a few dollars per person.

71 Bring/Get a Cooler

i Even if you don't go back to your room, by bringing a small cooler with you to the parks, (and store in a secure locker), you can bring your lunch with you. Disney permits small coolers (without wheels) into the Magic Kingdom, Epcot and Disney's Hollywood Studios. By "small," it is one that can fit into a locker, which is about 24"x17"x15".

ii Because of the live animals at Disney's Animal Kingdom Park, coolers are forbidden, and only soft bags like backpacks are allowed. If a guest has medication that needs refrigeration, Guest Relations can store it for you. Note that all coolers are subject to search, and cannot contain any glass containers or alcoholic beverages. Coolers are not allowed at Disney's golf courses, but each cart has its own which can be filled with ice. Larger coolers, including those with wheels, may also be brought into Disney's two water parks — Blizzard Beach and Typhoon Lagoon. If you have a car, you can purchase inexpensive Styrofoam or soft-side coolers at a nearby Walgreens, CVS, etc.

a. Guests are allowed to bring food items that do not require heating into any Walt Disney World Resort. No glass other than baby food jars can be brought in, but zip-top bags are a great way to store and transport food (and it makes getting through bag-check much faster, too!).

b. Don't want to lug your bag around? Rent a storage locker when you get to the parks and keep your cooler there until you need it.

iii **Bonus:** With all the money you saved on breakfast and lunch, consider indulging on a fancy dinner and celebrate your savings!

iv **Do Your Laundry.** On Vacation?? Oh the humanity!!! I know... you're on vacation and don't want to make your bed, think about cleaning the house, or do laundry. BUT, you can actually SAVE money on luggage costs (remember the airline baggage fees and weight limits!) by bringing fewer clothes and some laundry supplies from home and doing laundry once (or dare I say, twice) during your trip.

a. Bring or ship travel sized laundry detergent — you will save money on buying the detergent at Walt Disney

World, and is MUCH less expensive than sending your laundry out to be cleaned by Disney.

b. Plus... you can save room in your luggage for souvenirs! (Now that you're saving so much money, you can buy and bring back more!)

72 **Become a Member!!** No, not of the Mouseketeers, but of the Disney Vacation Club (DVC). If you plan to make Walt Disney World a regular, scheduled family vacation for many years to come, you may want to attend a presentation to learn more about this vacation ownership program.

i   DVC members purchase a specific number of vacation "points", which they can exchange for a variety of room types at a variety of Disney resorts throughout the year. Accommodations vary according to size, and their point value varies according to the time of year a family plans to travel (busier seasons require more points).

ii DVC properties (Disney's Old Key West Resort, Disney's Boardwalk Villas, Disney's Beach Club Villas, Disney's Villas at Wilderness Lodge, The Villas at Disney's Grand Floridian Resort & Spa, Disney's Saratoga Springs Resort & Spa, Disney's Animal Kingdom Villas and Disney's Bay Lake Tower Resort) offer a variety of rooming arrangements, from studio suites to spacious 1–3 bedroom villas.

a. Villas offer full kitchens, enabling guests to prepare their own meals and save on dining in the parks.

b. Washing machines and dryers are also in the vacation villas, enabling a family to save by doing their own laundry.

iii   DVC members are also eligible to add the Disney Dining Plan (see Dining Section) to their resort stay, saving up to 30% on their dining costs.

iv   Additional Discounts Available to Members:

     a.   There is a substantial savings on an annual pass. Currently, you can save approximately $100 off a basic Annual Pass and $125 off a premium Annual Pass.

     b.   Other DVC discounts include select dining discounts at table service restaurants across Disney property, theme park and resort tours, and discounts on various hard-ticketed events during Halloween and Christmas

     c.   Disney Vacation Club Members and up to 3 guests also receive discounts of 10%–20% (10% is more common) at many WDW restaurants, including many of the Downtown Disney and Swan/Dolphin restaurants. Does not apply to alcoholic beverages, tax or gratuities.

     d.   Do your research and make sure you fully understand the program when you attend a DVC presentation

73 Bring that large group to Suites/Villas —

i   You don't have to be DVC member to rent a DVC villa. You can pay cash for these accommodations — make sure to watch for other Disney discounts or promotions to make the most of your vacation dollar.

ii   For larger families, reunions or groups/get-togethers it may be cost effective to get a suite in one of the Disney Vacation Club one-, two-, or three-bedroom villas.

a. Resorts offer variable room layouts and numerous amenities.

b. Some larger properties allow for up to 12 guests to comfortably sleep, with plenty of room to spread out and enjoy a living area and kitchen.

74 Rent Disney Vacation Club points

i Sometimes, DVC members are unable to use their vacation points for a specific travel year and decide to rent their extra points to a non-DVC member.

ii A non-DVC member can arrange to rent the points for certain DVC resort properties at different times in the year, at a rate much less than it would be to pay cash for the rooms.

iii The savings in such an arrangement can be substantial, though you will likely need to be flexible in your travel dates and be willing to work with another Disney fan to make this arrangement beneficial for both parties.

STARTING YOUR DAY

75 Pack A BackPack

i OK, so I'm not a fanny pack guy, but I always bring a backpack or messenger bag to the parks. When I had infants, I also brought the requisite diaper bag, but whether you're going solo, with kids, or with just a bunch of friends, here are some items you should always pack in your backpack:

a. **Pack Snacks!** If you are visiting one of the Disney World theme parks with young children, don't forget to bring along some snacks. Snack item suggestions: Raisins, Cheerios, Goldfish, granola, trail mix (which you can make at home and bring in zip-top bags), cereal bars, energy bars for the adults, crackers (with peanut butter!), juice boxes, bananas, and grapes (in a zip-top bag)

b. **Water bottles (freeze 'em the night before and pack 'em with you)**

c. **Pens**

d. **Autograph books**

e. **Sunscreen/lip balm with good SPF protection**

f. **Sunglasses**
    (for the sun, not the paparazzi)

g. **Hat/cap**

h. **Hand sanitizer**

i. **Wet wipes**

j. **Ponchos** (from the "dollar store")

k. **Backup battery/charger for cell phone**

l. **Extra batteries and memory cards for your digital camera**

m. **Water spray bottle** (especially in the summer) to keep you and the kids cool

n. **Sweatshirt/light jacket/windbreaker.** It gets cool in Florida (no, seriously... it does), especially in the evenings during the winter months.

o.   **Tide pen** (for those accidental food and beverage spills)

p.   **Extra Ziploc bags** — one labeled WET and and one labeled DRY — If something gets wet, put it in the Wet bag (In the hotter Summer months, you can also put in a washcloth which you can run under cool water in the restroom and put on the back of your neck to stay cool). If you want to keep your cell phone dry on Splash Mountain or Kali River Rapids, put it in the Dry bag.

q.   **Aspirin/Ibuprofen/Bandages (just in case)**

76 **Order a Kids Meal** — Did you know that adults can order kids meals... without the kids? Some of the kids' meal sizes are large enough to feed an adult (especially for a small snack or light eaters). Some are even large enough for small children to split with an adult! For example, at some counter-service locations, you can order a child's breakfast platter for $4.99 that includes eggs, bacon, fruit and a drink!

i   **Bonus Tip:** Combine sides to make a meal! Another way to save is by ordering two sides instead of one meal. For example, at breakfast, you can get a bagel (side dish) with a side of bacon for about $5.00!

ii   **Note:** while cost-effective, this only works at counter service restaurants. Table-service restaurants do not allow adults to order off the children's menu

77 **Eat at the Store, Not the Restaurant** — Instead of eating at your resort's food court, stop in to the merchandise location first, as many have refrigerators with breakfast items like milk and juice for less than what you'll pay at the restaurant. For example, you can usually buy a quart of milk at the gift shop for just a little bit more than an 8-oz. carton in the food court.

EATING IN THE PARKS — When, Where, and How!

DID YOU KNOW? There is a Chinese Food restaurant on Main Street? Well, kinda. If you look at the second floor window above Casey's Corner, you'll see a sign for a Chinese Restaurant. It claims to sell Fine Foods and Imported Teas. "Jim Armstrong — Vegetable Buyer" is written below this pane, honoring a former cast member from the Food Services Division.

78 **Save on Character Meals — Two Tips:**

   i   *You Can Save: Almost $40 Per Meal — Family of 4 = $14 savings x2 + $10 savings x2 = $48*

   ii   **Save Your Character Meal For Breakfast or Lunch** — One of the best ways to save on these fun, interactive meals is to book them at breakfast or lunch. Why? Because they are priced much lower than the dinner meals! For example, at the Crystal Palace in Magic Kingdom, Pooh and his friends from the Hundred Acre Wood like Eeyore, Piglet and Tigger make their way around the restaurant greeting guests and leading children in a parade. This buffet meal experience is available for breakfast, lunch or dinner, but the breakfast is around $22.99 for adults ($12.99 per child) while dinner is $36.99 for an adult (plus tax) and children are $17.99 plus tax. *Note: Prices are subject to change and may also increase during peak seasons.*

iii **The Best Character Meal Value** can be found at the Garden Grove restaurant at the Walt Disney World Swan hotel. They offer a character breakfast on weekends (Saturday and Sundays only) for $23.99 for adults and $15.99 for kids. More importantly, there are a variety of characters, including Pluto and Goofy, and because the restaurant is generally not crowded, you can often get a reservation and spend a lot of time with the characters at your table. There is also a nightly character buffet six nights a week and a Friday evening seafood buffet as well! The Walt Disney World Swan is an easy walk from Disney's Boardwalk and Yacht and Beach Club Resorts, and can also be reached by boat from Epcot and Disney's Hollywood Studios. Not only that, no theme park admission is required! *(One caveat: if you drive to the Walt Disney World Swan, parking will cost you around $15 per vehicle)*

iv **Don't Splurge on a Character Breakfast** — Character meals are fun ways to let your kids (and you) meet their (your) favorite Disney characters at a more leisurely pace, as the characters will come right to your table, pose for photos and sign autographs. However, if you're looking to save money, consider eating a meal like breakfast in your room, and then taking the kids to Main Street, USA early in the morning, as characters are often scattered throughout the area posing for photos. Additionally, you can go "Backstage with Magician Mickey" and Minnie inside the Town Square Theater for pictures as well. Many of the characters you can meet in the restaurants can also be seen elsewhere throughout the day in the parks.

v   *Note that some characters can only be found in specific locations. For example, Cinderella can ONLY be found at Cinderella's Royal Table restaurant. If there's a specific character you're looking to meet, check your daily Times Guide at each theme park, as it includes character greeting times and locations.*

79 **Make Lunch Your Big Meal of the Day** — While many Counter-Service and Table-Service restaurants have consistent menus and prices for lunch and dinner, some Table-Service locations (such as Cinderella's Royal Table, Liberty Tree Tavern, Tony's Town Square Restaurant, many restaurants in World Showcase in Epcot, and some resort locations), have lunch menus with many of the same items that you can find on the dinner menus — but at a lower price!

i   So for example, if you were to dine at Sanaa at Disney's Animal Kingdom Lodge, you could get Tandoori Shrimp at lunch for about $6 less than the dinner item. By scheduling your lunch late in the afternoon, you can often make that your big meal of the day and have a great snack in the parks at night with the money you save!

ii   The same tip holds true for breakfast — have a late breakfast in the parks or at your resort (try a character meal!), and have a smaller, less expensive lunch or snack!

80   Skip the Table-Service Restaurants

You Can Save: $???????

ii   By eating at wide variety of counter-service locations, you can save both time AND money (and time IS money!). Why? Because counter service meals are generally less expensive than table-service restaurants, and because they are also less time-consuming, you have more time to spend having fun in the parks or around the resort. The food is just as delicious, equally as filling and there is an astounding array of choices!

iii   Some of my favorite table service locations that serve a wide variety of foods are listed below, along with hyperlinks to sample menus, where applicable.

a. **Magic Kingdom:**

- Quick Service: Pecos Bill Tall Tale Inn & Cafe

- Table Service: Be Our Guest or The Plaza (We had a great experience at the Plaza! Listen to WDW Radio Show 253 to share in what we discovered!)

b. **Epcot:**

- Quick Service: Katsura Grill in Japan, Tangierine Cafe in Morocco and Sunshine Seasons Food Fair

- Check out a live dining review of Katsura Grill in WDW Radio Show 270

- Table Service: Rose & Crown Dining Room (or Garden Grill in The Land)

c. **Disney's Hollywood Studios:**

- Quick Service: ABC Commissary (You can listen to a live dining review of the ABC Commissary on WDW Radio Show #278.)

- Table Service: Hollywood Brown Derby

d. **Disney's Animal Kingdom:**

- Quick Service: Flame Tree Barbeque

- Table Service: Yak & Yeti

e. **Downtown Disney:**

- Quick Service: Wolfgang Puck Express

- Table Service: House of Blues

f. For more information on the wide array of dining options available to you on Walt Disney World property, check out: Where to Eat: Dining & Reservations at Walt Disney World

81 **Save at non-Disney restaurants at Disney World** — Not every restaurant in Walt Disney World is owned and/or operated by Disney. In fact, there are many restaurants on property that offer some great savings and discounts!

i T-Rex Café (Downtown Disney) & Rainforest Café (outside Disney's Animal Kingdom entrance and at Downtown Disney) frequently offer free or reduced kids meals. By joining the Rainforest Café Safari Club for a one-time fee of $15, you can save 10% on food and merchandise, and get priority seating.

ii Restaurant.com has special gift certificates for select restaurants such as Il Mulino New York Trattoria, Shula's Steak House and Todd English's bluezoo inside the Walt Disney World Dolphin & Swan hotels — http://www.restaurant.com/chain/disneyswandolphinresort

82 Investigate Dinner Show Alternatives

i *You Can Save: More Than $100.00*

ii The Hoop-Dee-Doo Musical Revue is an old-fashioned dinner show at Pioneer Hall in Disney's Fort Wilderness Resort & Campground that is good, ol' country fun for the whole family. But, it can be pricey, especially if you have a large family or group. A great alternative is to visit the Whispering Canyon Café at Disney's Wilderness Lodge. Located in one of the most elaborately-themed resorts in Walt Disney World, the

Whispering Canyon Café also provides a lively, fun experience at a more affordable price.

a. **Sample Savings**: The Hoop-Dee-Doo Musical Revue has tiered pricing by category that varies depending on the time of year. It can range between $55–$67 per adult, and $28–25 per child.

b. With menu items at the Whispering Canyon Café ranging from around $16 to $31 per adult, and kids meals that include an option for "Kids' Complete Meals" ($8.99 gets a child an appetizer, entree, dessert and drink) a family of four can easily save over $100!

iii The Spirit of Aloha Dinner Show is an enchanting and exotic evening with family entertainment and delicious, polynesian-themed, all-you-care-to-eat food and drink, located on the grounds of the Polynesian Resort. While attending this dinner can be the highlight of a family vacation, tickets can start at $73.99 for adults and $39.99 for children, making it a big ticket part of your vacation budget. A great alternative is Ohana, an all-you can eat Hawaiian feast with fun family entertainment and inspiring views of the Magic Kingdom. Adults dine for up to $39.40 and kids for up to $19.16. This is a substantial savings over the Spirit of Aloha dinner show.

83 **Make-Your-Own Fireworks Dessert Party!** — Disney offers a wonderful experience in the Magic Kingdom with their Tomorrowland Terrace Fireworks Dessert Party. Ranging from $15 to $35.99 per person (prices are subject to change), guests get a special private dessert party with a wonderful vantage point for Wishes® Nighttime Spectacular fireworks show from the Tomorrowland Terrace Restaurant.

i   Want to save some money but still have a special fireworks experience? Visit Disney's Polynesian Resort, and grab a Dole Whip, snack, or drink from Capt. Cooks and watch both Wishes® Nighttime Spectacular fireworks in the Magic Kingdom from the beach of the Polynesian! And remember — there's no theme park admission required!

ii   Extra Bonus — You'll not only get to see the fireworks from a unique vantage point, but you'll also get an additional show — the Electrical Water Pageant — and you don't have to worry about the crowds leaving the park!

84 **Dine at a Not-So-Hidden Treasure — Earl Of Sandwich —** Located in the Downtown Disney Marketplace, it is one of the very best values (and meals!) in Walt Disney World. Here, you can get a full meal of a sandwich, side and drink for only around $10 per person! Check out their menu at EarlOfSandwichUSA.com

85 **Skip the Sides**

i   *You Can Save: Around $8.00 Per Meal*

ii   When eating at a counter-service location, did you know you can skip the sides to save money? Even though the restaurants list complete meals on the menus, you don't have to order a combination! For example, want the burger without the fries or the sandwich without the vegetable or chips? Just ask! You'll pay only for the burger or sandwich, and so by ordering what they want, a family of 4 could save up to $2 per person or $8 per meal! *Note that this only applies to adult meals, as kids' kids' meals are sold as a package.*

86   Request Free Ice Water

i   *You Can Save: More Than $145.00 on Soda Alone!*

ii   While bringing your own bottle for water from the fountains is one option, did you know that you can ask for FREE ice water when ordering food from counter service restaurants? Remember that not only does water quench your thirst better than soda, but drinking water instead of soda also can save you a considerable amount of money! A regular soda costs about $2.59, so if everyone in a family of four drinks water instead of two sodas per day on a seven-day vacation, that's a savings of more than $145 on soda alone!

iii   Want more flavor than plain water? Remember to pack some small packets of powdered mixers.

87   Save Money At Table Service Restaurants — HOW you eat can save you money as well.

i   **Apps (not the mobile phone kind)** — One of my favorite ways to dine in Walt Disney World can also be a big money-saver as well. How? By skipping the entrée. Ordering (and sharing among friends) a variety of appetizers and desserts is a great way to sample many different food items and get a full meal without spending $20-30 for an entrée.

   a.   One of my personal favorites is also a Walt Disney World "hidden treasure" — Eating at the bar/lounge at Sanaa at Disney's Animal Kindgom Lodge.

   b.   I also had a fabulous time trying this strategy at Disney's Wilderness Lodge. Check out my live review!

ii **Split It —** Two people can also split an entrée at most table-service restaurants (though some restaurants not owned/operated by Disney may charge you for an additional plate) Some of my favorite options for sharing are listed below (please note, prices are subject to change.)

a. Sunshine Seasons in the Land Pavilion at Epcot-order a half rotisserie chicken or other meats with one side (split it between two people) for $11. Add an additional side for just $2–3. This comes to approximately $20 with drinks for 2 people. Add a soup for roughly $4.

b. San Angel Inn Restaurante This table service dining location in the Mexico Pavilion at Epcot has large lunch portions, that are reasonably priced. Families of 4 could buy 2 entrees, 2 appetizers & 2 desserts and then share.

c. 50's Primetime Cafe A table service location in Disney's Hollywood Studios, there are many reasonably priced entrees that can be shared, including a "Sampling of Mom's Favorite Recipes." This $20.99 entree includes fried chicken, pot roast, and meatloaf, and can happily be shared. (And if you clean the plate, Ma will be happy!)

d. Flame Tree Barbecue This Animal Kingdom eatery has a half smoked chicken with two sides (split it between two people) for about $10.

e. Pollo Campero This quick service location at Downtown Disney offers a family dinner of fried chicken, rice and pintos with some plantains — it's more than enough to feed 3 people.

f. There are many other locations where you may be able to share an entree. A lot depends upon your family's dining habits and preferences. As always, research and planning will help you to know the best way to maximize your options.

iii The Same... for less! Sometimes you can get the same food from a table-service restaurant, but at a counter-service location (and for a lower price!).

a. For example, Captain Cook's, located on the ground floor of Disney's Polynesian's Resort Grand Ceremonial House, is a delightful quick service food court with an array of family friendly dining options. Here, you can order the world famous Tonga Toast, a sumptuous, melt-in-your-mouth version of French toast that is stuffed with bananas. This fabled Disney meal also is served upstairs at the Kona Cafe. Kona Cafe serves Tonga Toast with a side of breakfast meat for $12.99 (plus tax and tip). At Captain Cook's, Tonga Toast is served by itself for $4.49 plus tax.

b. Liberty Tree Tavern in the Magic Kingdom — a bowl of New England Clam Chowder is $6.99 at lunch. Get the same chowder at the nearby Columbia Harbour House for $4.49 a bowl.

c. Hollywood Brown Derby at Disney's Hollywood Studios — Flourless Chocolate Cake is served with sorbet on the side for $8 (plus tax and tip). At the Starring Rolls bakery next door, you can get a slice of the same cake (without garnish) for under $3.

d. Zebra Domes desserts, made famous at the Boma buffet at Disney's Animal Kingdom Lodge ($25.99 for an adult meal), can be purchased a la carte at the Mara food court near the pool for just $3.69 each. Also, some of the delicious soups served at Boma can also be purchased here for just $2.49 per bowl.

e. Rose and Crown Pub in Epcot serves fish and chips for $15.99 (plus tax and tip). A smaller portion of the same fish and chips (without a side of peas) can be purchased next door at Yorkshire County Fish Shop for $7.99 plus tax.

102
WAYS
TO SAVE MONEY
FOR AND AT
WALT DISNEY WORLD

BY LOU MONGELLO

SHOPPING

88 **Establish a Souvenir Budget — And Stick to It! —** BEFORE
you leave home, establish a budget for yourself (and your kids)
for souvenirs and stick to it. Set a daily budget or dollar amount
for the entire trip. Put it aside (see how to limit your spending
by using Disney Gift Cards on your trip and don't go over it. This
helps teach kids the value of money, and the idea of saving for
the next day or the next vacation. For example, here are some
commonly-purchased souvenirs and their current price at time
of publication:

- **Mickey Ears:** $13.95

- **T-Shirt:** From $12.50 for youth; $16.50 for adults

- **Ladies' handbag:** from $16.95 for non-name brand purses. Disney carries LeSportSac and Dooney & Bourke bags, which are considerably more expensive

- **Disney pin trading** — from $6.95 per pin. A pin trading starter set (which includes a lanyard and 4 pins — 2 each of 2 different pins — runs $24.95 and is a fun way to introduce your children to this fun Disney tradition.

- **Mickey plush** — 18 inch — $19.50

- **Magnet** — $4.95–$10.95

- **Christmas Ornament** — $9.95–$24.95 (Some locations will add beautiful personalization to your ornament, from $3. But don't wait too long! There can be significant wait times for the personalization.)

89 Shop Before You Shop

i **You Can Save: $10.00–200.00 Per Visit**

ii Shop at home before you go and purchase the essentials such as batteries, memory cards, aspirin, diapers, sunscreen, etc. before you arrive at Walt Disney World. You'll save versus buying these items inside the theme parks.

iii   You can also "pre-purchase" souvenirs at the online Disney Store outlet and present the kids with t-shirts, plush animals, and other merchandise. You could even have "Tinkerbell" visit your hotel room each night and leave these small gifts on the children's suitcases. This curbs the need to purchase souvenirs and saves money, too!

iv   Disney Store Online now carries select Disney Theme Park merchandise. If you carefully observe online sales, you can purchase what you would have bought and save money, too! There is a sale tab on the site where clearance merchandise is featured.

v   The Target dollar bins often have Disney-licensed merchandise you can purchase (notepads, crayons, storybooks) that will satisfy the need for a "take home."

vi   Plan for the last day of the trip to be "souvenir day." During the other days of your trip, all members of the party can look at the souvenirs available and think about what they most would like to take home. Take pictures of items you are considering and email them to yourself with a note indicating where the item can be found. This way, you can efficiently purchase the "most wanted" items!

90 Bring Your Own Stroller

i   *You Can Save: Around $15.00–$30.00 Per Day*

ii   Although you can rent a stroller in all of the Walt Disney World theme parks (http://disneyworld.disney.go.com/guest-services/stroller-rentals), there are advantages and cost-savings to bringing your own. By purchasing an inexpensive umbrella stroller (either bring one from home, have one shipped to your resort from Walmart, or get one from a local Walgreens, CVS, etc.), you will save on multi-day rentals in the parks. Additionally, the Disney strollers can not be brought out of the parks, so if your child is tired at the end of the day, guess who is carrying him/her to the monorail or bus and back to your room? Don't want to schlep the stroller back home? Pay it forward by giving it a quick cleaning and giving it to a family that may want to use it before you leave your resort.

91 **Save on Disney's Rental Strollers** — If you don't want to bring or buy your own stroller, you can save on renting a stroller from Disney in the parks. If you need a stroller (single or double) for multiple days, Disney offers a "length of stay rental ticket" which allows you to make a one-time payment transaction for as many days of rental as you will need. When you visit a Disney Theme Park, just show your receipt at the stroller rental location and you will get your stroller quickly and without having to go through the rental process over and over again (remember — time is money!)

92 **Bring (or Make!) Your Own Autograph Books** — Walgreens, Walmart, and many grocery stores in the Orlando area have officially-licensed Disney autograph books which are less expensive than the ones in the parks and resorts. Better yet — have some fun and make your own at home before you go! It's a great craft for the kids that helps them get excited about the trip! Buy a small, spiral notebook at your local craft or dollar store, get some Disney or scrapbooking stickers and voila! You have your own, custom autograph book! (Be sure and bring a Sharpie with you to make it easier for the characters to sign your books!)

i   As an alternative to an autograph book, you can affordably purchase a picture frame mat and have characters autograph that. THEN, print a picture from your vacation and place it in this unique frame!

ii Another autograph option is to combine a souvenir with an autograph book. Do you collect Vinylmations? Purchase a 9" blank ("Create Your Own") Vinylmation and have the characters sign it. Now you have a one-of-a kind collectible! Make sure you mark the date of your Vinylmation on the bottom!

93   Bring Your Own Poncho

i   *You Can Save: $20.00 — ($6 per poncho per person for family of 4 vs. $1 each at Dollar Store)*

ii Let's just get this out of the way right now — depending on when you visit Walt Disney World, there's a good chance it may rain. But here's the good news — it will probably only rain for about 20 minutes or so and then it's done. Better news? Don't wait for it to rain to buy a poncho in Walt Disney World. Instead, visit your local dollar discount store before you leave home, and pack everyone in the family their own poncho. They're easier to carry than umbrellas and act as a good "insurance policy" in case it rains.

iii Wait... you think you can't have fun in Walt Disney World when it rains? Check out my show covering the **Top Ten Things To Do in Walt Disney World When It Rains** — http://WDWRadio.com/rain

94 Disney's PhotoPass CD

i   Disney's PhotoPass is a wonderful, FREE service that will help you capture all of your vacation memories AND still be in all of the pictures! How? Disney PhotoPass photographers can be found throughout the parks and resorts, often in wonderful photo locations (in front of Cinderella Castle, Spaceship Earth, attractions, character meet-and-greet locations, etc.). Simply ask to have your photo taken, and the photographer will hand you a complimentary Disney PhotoPass Card. Keep it throughout your vacation and give it to a PhotoPass Photographer every time they take your picture. When you return home from vacation, you can visit http://www.DisneyPhotoPass.com, register for free, and enter the ID number on your card. Then, you can view all your photos online, (and even upload some of your own) for 30 days after your trip is over! You can then customize them and order prints, photo books, mugs and other keepsakes.

ii   But wait... there's more! It's called **PhotoPass+** — In April, 2012, Disney introduced PhotoPass+, an all-inclusive package with all your PhotoPass photos PLUS select attraction photos AND Dining Print Packages *(taken within a 14 day visit)*, all for $199.95! It includes:

   a.   A voucher to exchange for your Disney PhotoPass+ card

   b.   Disney's Photo Gallery CD with hundreds of stock photos

   c.   A unique code to create and order a Photo CD ($169.95 value)

   d.   Print packages at select dining locations ($29.95 each if purchased separately)

e. Digital photos from select attractions ($14.95 each if purchased separately)

f. But here's my favorite money-saving tip! Remember that you can load up the card with as many photos as you like — there's no limit, so let the Photographers snap away! But by PRE-ORDERING your CD **BEFORE** you leave on vacation, you can get all of your photos on a Photo CD for $119.95! (Currently $169.95 if purchased after your vacation). Simply visit Disney's PhotoPass Previsit Offer page to take advantage of the savings at http://www.disneyphotopass.com/previsitoffer.aspx

DID YOU KNOW? The largest merchandise store in any of the four Walt Disney World theme parks is Mouse Gear, located in Epcot.

WHERE AND HOW TO SHOP

95 Check those receipts!

i   *You Can Save: Up to 20% Off Merchandise*

ii Walt Disney World Resort restaurant receipts sometimes offer 10–20% discounts on merchandise at select Disney stores throughout the park. Usually, they require you to shop early in the day, so remember to use your free package delivery service so you can enjoy the rides for the rest of the day!

96 **Inexpensive Collectibles and Souvenirs** — Disney souvenirs don't have to be expensive! There are a number of highly-sought-after mementos and fun ways to preserve your Disney vacation memories. Some these include:

i   **Pressed Pennies** — Our kids LOVE getting pressed pennies from any destination we go to, especially Disney. Pressed penny collections are fun, family-friendly, and inexpensive collectibles that document a trip through Walt Disney World. Here are some strategies for making these small collectibles a treasured activity.

a.   **M&M tubes!**

- Buy one for each child in the family. Eat the M&Ms, peel off the label, and the kids decorate the tube with their name, stickers, etc.

- Organize the coins (2 quarters and one penny, 2 quarters one penny, until it's full!)

- Attach yarn to the bottles so we carry them easily!

- Bring a zip top baggie for all the pressed pennies!

- **Hint:** So you don't spend your entire vacation at pressed penny machines, establish ground rules or themes. "We will only get a pressed penny at restaurants where we actually eat" or "we only get pressed pennies for attractions we actually experience." There are easily hundreds of pressed penny options out there, so don't try to do it all!

b.   **Another alternative:** Disney offers inexpensive pressed penny books in which a child can display pressed pennies. This would make a fun souvenir that you can add to with each successive Disney vacation!

ii   **Antenna Toppers** — Whether you have an antenna on your car or not (or even if you don't have a car!), Disney character antenna toppers are a great collectible and come in literally hundreds of different characters, Mickey heads, designs and themes. Antenna toppers generally cost only around $4.95 each, and can be put on display at home or put one on your car's antenna (great for helping you find your car in the parking lot... and the toppers are a recognizable symbol to fellow Disney fans!)

iii **Magnets** — Disney magnets can be found for under $5.00 throughout the parks and resorts. They are wonderful collectibles and keepsakes from your visit. They can be used to hang your children's artwork on your refrigerator, or collect your favorite character, attraction, or theme!

iv   **Buttons** — Usually located near the checkout register at many Walt Disney World merchandise locations, you can find a small, clear container of mini-buttons. Smaller than the size of a quarter, they feature a wide variety of characters and designs and are much less expensive than the Disney pins. You can purchase a few buttons for under $5.00

v   **Mini-Collectible Figures** — The Disney Parks Collectors Packs each include 3 collectible mini character figures that stand around 1 inch tall. Purchase a sealed bag of figures for around $6.95 and open it to see what you get, as each pack is a surprise! There are a number of different Series, including numerous Theme Park series, Pirates of the Caribbean, Star Wars, Holidays and others. Each series has 18 figures to collect, mix and match with other collector pack figures. They are fun to collect, trade and display, and the fact that they are inexpensive and extremely portable makes them an idea collectible souvenir!

97 **Disney Pins! — *Trade* for Disney pins, instead of purchasing them!**

   i   Disney Pin Collecting is an incredibly popular past-time. Cast members all around the parks wear lanyards on which they have pins they are willing to trade for other Disney pins. Purchasing pins can get pricey at an average cost of $6.95 to $12.95 and more.

   ii   If you believe you will want to be involved in pin trading, consider purchasing less expensive pins in advance of your trip and trading cast members to get pins you like.

       a.   Pins can be purchased in lots at a reduced cost on eBay

       b.   "Tradeable" pins are Disney pins that are enamel or enamel cloisonné with a metal base and a Disney copyright engraved on the back. At least one cast member in every park or resort merchandise shop will have a lanyard of pins and will be happy to trade.

       c.   If you don't see a cast member with a pin lanyard, ask at the cash register. Often, stocks of pins are kept under the counter for those who wish to trade.

98 **Shop at area factory outlet stores** such as Orlando Premium Outlets, which sells Disney merchandise at significantly lower prices than you will find at stores within the Disney World theme parks. There are 2 official Disney Outlet stores in the Walt Disney

World Area (not located within Disney property). They each carry a wide selection of discounted Disney merchandise. Selections vary between stores and throughout the year.

i   Disney's Character Warehouse at the Orlando Premium Outlet Vineland Avenue — 8200 Vineland Avenue, Orlando, FL 32821 (407) 477-0222

ii   Disney's Character Warehouse at Orlando Premium Outlet International — 4951 International Drive, Orlando, FL 32819 (407) 354-3255

iii   Character Outlet — Lake Buena Vista Factory Stores — 15591 State Road 535, Orlando, FL 32821 (407) 238-9301

SPECIAL EXPERIENCES AND EVENTS

99 **Consider** Bibbidi Bobbidi Boutique **or** Pirates League **Alternatives**

i   The Bibbidi Bobbidi Boutique is a wonderland for the aspiring Disney princess. Complete with a personalized fairy godmother, young damsels can have their hair, make-up, and nails done to bring out their inner Disney princess.

ii   Likewise, for those of us aspiring to be a swashbuckling pirate, Disney offers the chance to become a buccaneer — complete with make-up and a pirate oath!

iii   Both these experiences, while magical Disney experiences, can be quite expensive for a family on a tight budget. *(The starting price for the Boutique is $54.95 and for the Pirates League is $29.95)*

iv   As an alternative, consider visiting the Harmony Barber Shop for glitter and hair paint. For those receiving their first haircut, a special experience is offered as well. Reservations can be made (avoid the frequently LONG wait) by calling 407-WDW-DINE.

v   Pre-purchase glitter or hair paint at your local party store. Paint a Mickey silhouette on the back (or side) of their hair and add some glitter! Voila! You did it!! Kids won't indulge in the salon-style experience, but you WILL have more time to enjoy the attractions!

vi   Bring your own costume! Whether you have an aspiring princess or pirate, consider purchasing clothing and props at home and bringing it along for the trip. You can always visit a local party store after Halloween and purchase discount costumes. You can "plus" the costume by purchasing a small Disney prop (a Captain Jack sword or Cinderella wand).

100 **Sit Back, Relax, and Enjoy a Movie** — The AMC Downtown Disney 24, offers Guests the latest movies in state-of-the-art theaters, as well as dining and more. It's a wonderful way to enjoy a relaxing time outside the parks, and is a great option for a rainy day. Featuring loveseat-style stadium seating with the THX Surround Sound and Sony Dynamic Digital Sound, the 24-theatre complex resembles an Art Deco movie house of the 1920s, but with all the modern amenities, including one of the first Enhanced Theater Experience (ETX™) in the United States, featuring a 20% larger, floor-to-ceiling screen, 3D technology and 12 channel audio and digital projection that delivers higher resolution than HD. You can also experience the Dine-In Theatre and enjoy your favorite foods and cocktails with seat-side service. MacGuffins

Bar and Lounge is a great place to relax before or after the show for cocktails and conversation. Walt Disney World Annual and Seasonal Passholders receive $2.00 off adult evening admission price 7 days a week after 6pm. Offer is valid for the Passholder only and not valid with any other offer or discount.

BEFORE YOU LEAVE

101 **Resort Hop!** Take an afternoon before the end of your vacation and visit some other Disney resort hotels. Think about the perks of your current location and what you wish had been different. By checking out some other resorts, you can enjoy their theming and story, and also plan your budget for your next trip.

102 Book another Vacation... Before This Vacation Is Over... (and save!)

i *You Can Save: Up to 45% at a Walt Disney World Resort*

ii If you are staying at a Walt Disney World Resort, Disney sometimes will give **"Bounce Back"** to guests. This allows you to "bounce back" to Walt Disney World by booking your next vacation at a discounted price before this one is over.

iii When a "Bounce Back" offer is available, you can book a discounted room-only stay on selected dates at a Walt Disney World resort, but ONLY before you check out of your current stay. *(Note that there are some blackout dates and not all resorts and room types may be available)*

iv To book, simply call the number provided (located on a flyer in your room) or visit the resort's Front Desk, and pay a one-night deposit when booking. If you don't see a flyer in your room, just ask at the Front Desk if any offer is available.

102
WAYS
TO SAVE MONEY
FOR AND AT
WALT DISNEY WORLD

BY LOU MONGELLO

BONUS!

40 FREE THINGS TO DO, GET, SEE, EAT AND COLLECT!

This bonus section will illuminate some free ways to build an even more magical vacation for you and your family. In addition to these tips, be sure to listen to WDW Radio Show #153, The Best Free and Low Cost Things to Do in the Parks!

BEFORE YOU GO

1   **Get a FREE Walt Disney World Vacation Planning DVD!!!** By visiting http://DisneyVacations.com, you can order a FREE DVD directly from Disney to help plan and prepare for your next Walt Disney World vacation. Your DVD will include a complete tour of the 4 Theme Parks, 2 Water Parks and over 20 Resort hotels at the Walt Disney World® Resort, a tour of the Disneyland® Resort in California, tips on affordable ways to play and stay during your Disney vacation, pocket-sized planning guides, planning tips, and information on special events! *(Offer only available to U.S. and Canadian households)*

2   **Free Customized Maps** — Planning is part of the fun and Disney will send you not one but **five** full-color, keepsake-quality, 14" x 20" customized maps of the Walt Disney World Resort, as well as a set of golden stickers to mark your favorite park locations! You can customize your map to add your favorite attractions, choose a theme, add your upcoming vacation plans and more! Visit http://customizedmaps.disney.go.com to get your free maps!

3 Crafty Tip: **Turn the Free Maps into Autograph Books** — Bring your maps with a Sharpie marker and have your favorite characters autograph them! When you get home, you have a special souvenir of the attractions you visited along with the Disney friends you met along the way!

WHEN YOU'RE THERE

IN THE RESORT HOTELS — Even if you are not staying IN the specific Disney Resort hotel described, you can enjoy some of the classic Disney entertainment and services.

4 **Stroll around Disney's Boardwalk** — Disney's Boardwalk is an entertainment district themed after 20th century boardwalks made famous in places like Atlantic City, New Jersey and Coney Island, New York. Disney's Boardwalk contains more than 90,000 square feet of shops, restaurants and nightclubs. It is located on Crescent Lake and is within walking distance of many resorts, including Disney's Boardwalk, Disney's Yacht & Beach Club Resorts, and the Walt Disney World Swan and Dolphin. It is also a short walk from Epcot and Disney's Hollywood Studios, and free water taxi transportation from the parks is available as well. There is no admission and anyone is welcome to enjoy the shopping, dining options, and live entertainment. Street performers including magicians, jugglers and musicians entertain guests of all ages most evenings from approximately 6:00–10:00pm.

    i **Other fun things to do on Disney's Boardwalk include:**

        a. Play the carnival-style games (available at a small cost)

        b. Rent (at a small cost) a surrey bike for up to four people

        c. Visit the ESPN Zone arcade

d. Grab a snack, enjoy the background music and watch the Friendship Boats ply the waterways of Crescent Lake (**Lou's Tip** — I love doing this early in the morning. Grab a coffee and a delicious treat from the Boardwalk Bakery and relax while enjoying the music, scenery and sunrise)

e. At night, adults can visit Jellyrolls — a fun, lively dueling piano bar with audience sing-a-longs (21 and over, with a $10.00 cover charge). To enjoy bands and DJs, Guests 21 years and older can dance the night away at the majestic art deco ballroom of the Atlantic Dance Hall nightclub — with NO cover charge!

5 **Free Mickey Wake Up Call** — If you're staying at a Walt Disney World Resort, a great way to start your kids' (or your own) day is with a wake-up call from Mickey Mouse! Simply request a wake-up call from your resort room phone and Mickey (or one of his pals) will give you a wonderful wake-up message!

i **Bonus Tip:** Are you celebrating a birthday, anniversary or special event? You can also schedule a voicemail during your visit. Just tell the Cast Member during the reservation process or when you arrive at your resort, and a complimentary Disney character voicemail will be left on your room phone!

6 **Explore the Resorts** — Each of the Walt Disney World resort hotels is incredibly well-themed, and each tells their own unique story. There are plenty of things to see, do and enjoy (for free!) while you're there, so take some time to visit and explore them all! Use complimentary Disney transportation to visit!

i To get an idea of the amazing storytelling you can enjoy at the resorts, check out these WDW Radio Shows:

a. Show #208: The History Stories, and Details of the Wilderness Lodge.

b. Show #97: A DSI ("Disney Scene Investigation") of Port Orleans Resort

ii **Bonus Tip:** If you're traveling by your own car and visiting and Magic Kingdom resorts, enter the Magic Kingdom toll booth on the right side and let the attendant know that you are not going to the park, but visiting the resort and you will not have to pay a parking fee.

7 Free Sing-Along at Disney's Fort Wilderness Resort:

i You and your family can gather around the campfire at Disney's Fort Wilderness Resort with along with your pals Chip & Dale. Each night starting at 7:00 pm (in fall and winter and about 8:00 pm in spring and summer — weather permitting), a "Park Ranger" leads everyone around the campfire in song. You can roast marshmallows (available for purchase at the Chuckwagon or bring your own) and then watch a Disney movie on the large, outdoor screen — all for free! This experience is open to all Walt Disney World resort guests. The campfire is located near the Meadow Trading Post. No reservations necessary.

ii · **Bonus Tip:** During the holidays, Fort Wilderness guests often decorate their campsites in Disney style! Lights and inflatable figurines make an already festive environment even more fun!

8 Campfire and a Disney Movie

i You can find campfires and movies at other Walt Disney World resorts (without characters) as well. Weather permitting, many resorts show movies in the evening by the pool or on the beach (e.g. Disney's Polynesian Resort and Disney's Yacht & Beach Club Resort). These are free and open to all Walt Disney World resort guests — simply call or stop by the resort's front desk to find out what movie is playing. Marshmallow s'mores kits are available for purchase at the campfire as well.

a. Port Orleans offers a "Campfire on de' Bayou" or "Cajun Campfire" with stories, sing-alongs and s'mores. It is behind the Muddy Rivers pool bar on Ol' Man Island, next to the children's playground.

b. Disney's Port Orleans French Quarter's "Cajun Campfire" takes places in the courtyard behind building 6 overlooking the Sassagoula River. While there are no characters in attendance, it is free to all Walt Disney World resort guests.

9   **Free Tours!**

i   Several deluxe Walt Disney World resorts, including Animal Kingdom Lodge, Wilderness Lodge, Grand Floridian, and Yacht Club, offer FREE tours that are open to any Disney resort guest (whether you are staying at that particular hotel or not). Some of the tours require a reservation, so inquire in advance or at the resort's front desk.

10   **Watch the Polynesian Torch-Lighting Ceremony** — On Tuesday through Saturday evenings at 6:00 pm, a fire-dancer from the "Spirit of Aloha Polynesian Luau" dinner show enters the Great Ceremonial House at Disney's Polynesian Resort to perform the traditional "Torch Lighting Ceremony." After blowing on a conch shell to begin the ritual, guests can follow him outside to witness him spin a baton of fire and light some of the torches that line the pathways throughout the resort. The short performance is fun to watch, is often an unexpected surprise, and is unique to this resort.

11   **Free Hula Lessons** — As long as we're at Disney's Polynesian Resort... when in the South Pacific... Let's hula! Complimentary hula lessons take place most days inside the Great Ceremonial House lobby. The classes take place Monday through Saturday at 3:45pm, and on Saturday mornings from 10:00am until 12:00pm.

i   "Auntie Kaui," a hula dancer and instructor with more than 50 years of experience, usually leads the classes, which can be enjoyed by kids and adults. The afternoon classes are generally geared more towards kids (who can wear leis and grass skirts), while the weekend classes are for guests of all ages. While the Saturday class lasts two hours, you are free to come and go as you like. Oh... and bring your camera!

12   **Go on a Nighttime Safari** — Visiting Disney's Animal Kingdom Lodge during the day affords you the opportunity to view animals roaming the savannah... but did you know you could also see them at night? Walk through the lobby to the outdoor viewing areas by the fire pit and you can borrow (at no cost) night vision goggles from the Cast Member to see exotic African animals roaming the savannah.

13   **Storytelling At The Animal Kingdom Lodge**

    i   Listen to the storyteller nightly at the fire pit at Arusha Rock outside the lobby

    ii   The storyteller spins tales of Africa for both kids and adults

    iii   In the event of inclement weather, storytelling is held inside the lobby.

    iv   Check with the front desk at Disney's Animal Kingdom Lodge for times

14   **Bob Jackson at Disney's Port Orleans Riverside Resort** — The River Roost Lounge at Disney's Port Orleans Riverside Resort Lounge offers Southern hospitality at its finest, with comfortable fireside chairs, spacious seating area, and bar for drinks and appetizers. But the real reason to visit is to see, hear and sing along with one of Walt Disney World's true hidden treasures — YeHaa Bob Jackson.

    i   Completely kid-friendly, Bob performs a fun, energetic sing-along show at his trademark rockin' piano. Bob meets and greets guests before the show, and gets them involved in the action (don't feel like singing? That's OK. There are plenty of other ways to get involved, or just sit back and enjoy the performance).

ii   Bob usually appears Tuesday through Saturday nights from 8:30pm until Midnight. There is no cover charge at the Lounge or to see Bob. He posts his schedule on his website at YehaaBob.com. I promise this will be some of the most fun you can have while in Walt Disney World in a can't-miss show. Like Bob says, "No one has more fun than us!!!"

iii   Check out a video of part of one of YehaaBob's shows!

15   **Not Ready to Leave Yet? Store Your Luggage for a While** — Unfortunately, every Walt Disney World vacation eventually comes to an end (there's never enough time, is there?). But let's say that checkout time is at 11:00 a.m., but your flight isn't until 8:00 p.m. that evening. Did you know that you can leave your luggage at your resort's Bell Services desk? They will keep your bags in a climate-controlled, secure location until you're ready to leave for the airport — at no charge to you!

i   **Bonus Tip:** Can't bear to leave so you decide to extend your vacation or switch resorts mid-trip? If you're switching between Walt Disney World resort hotels during your visit, Bell Services will gladly move your luggage between resorts for you for free!

16   **Celebrate Spring!** During the Easter holidays, many resorts host candy scrambles and free egg hunts for children. In the past, egg hunts also have been held in different parks. Easter eggs have been known to pop up in unique places and can have a variety of prizes included! Characters dressed in springtime gear are often available during these events as well.

17   **Pool Parties!** Many resorts host daily events by the pool — from dance parties to scavenger hunts to hula hoop contests, the fun is endless! Some resorts also offer shuffleboard, basketball, tennis, as well as craft activities for kids and the family. Be sure to read your check-in materials for resort activities at the pool and throughout the resort.

18   **Music In Disney's Grand Floridian Resort & Spa Lobby**

i   Depending on time/day of the week — either a magnificent pianist or The Grand Floridian Society Orchestra can be found playing in the lobby of this magnificent deluxe resort.

ii   The music lends to the breathtaking atmosphere, making this an elegant, cool place to relax, unwind, and breathe in the majesty of Disney story-telling.

iii   The Pianist in the lobby, whose CD you can purchase in Sandy Cove, starts playing at 3 p.m. and alternates with the orchestra until 9:45 p.m.

AT DOWNTOWN DISNEY

Once known as the Lake Buena Vista Village, Downtown Disney (located near Disney's Saratoga Springs Resort & Spa) has things to do (many of them free!) for the entire family. From daytime fun to exciting nightlife, there's something for everyone from dining to shopping to interactive activities and more! *Follow Downtown Disney on Twitter* — *http://twitter. com/WDWDowntown*

In March, 2013, Walt Disney World Resort announced plans for a multi-year transformation of Downtown Disney into Disney Springs, which will treat guests to more shopping, dining and entertainment, nestled within beautiful open-air promenades, meandering springs and charming waterfront district. Disney Springs will double the number of shops, restaurants and other venues, resulting in more than 150 establishments. It will include four outdoor neighborhoods including the Town Center, Marketplace, The Landing, and West Side, which will be connected by a flowing spring. Disney Springs is expected to be complete in 2016

19   Admission and parking at Downtown Disney is complimentary, so it's easy to visit via your own car or free Disney transportation from your resort. It's also a short walk from Disney's Saratoga Springs resort & Spa or any of the Downtown Disney Resort Area Hotels — http://DowntownDisneyHotels.com

    i   Downtown Disney is divided into 3 Areas:

        a. **Downtown Disney West Side**, features the House of Blues, AMC® Downtown Disney 24 movie theater,

La Nouba™ by Cirque du Soleil®, DisneyQuest® Indoor Interactive theme park as well as other shopping and dining options

b. **Pleasure Island** is home to unique dining experiences at restaurants such as Raglan Road™ Irish Pub & Restaurant, Portobello, Paradiso 37 and Fulton's Crab House, as well as a variety of shops and entertainment

c. **Downtown Disney Marketplace** is a shopping mecca, with a wide variety of shops including Art of Disney, Once Upon a Toy Store, World of Disney and numerous unique boutique locations.

20 **Free Entertainment** — There is often free outdoor entertainment at the Marketplace Waterside Stage, where schools from around the country are often invited to showcase their singing or dancing performances. At night, a DJ spins records (well, not really records, but...) so you can get up and dance or sing along. The open-air theater has a large seating area so it's often a nice place to sit, relax and enjoy a free show.

i   House of Blues, located on the Downtown Disney West Side, often has free live music on its Front Porch Bar. Kids are welcome (to watch and listen, but alcoholic drinks are for guests 21 and over, of course).

ii Step into the authentic Raglan Road Irish Pub and Restaurant for nightly entertainment (usually beginning around 6:00pm), featuring award-winning Irish dancers and Creel, the house band that performs traditional Irish music. RaglanRoad.com

21 **Seasonal Activities** — Throughout the year, Downtown Disney is home to fun, family-friendly events that are free and feature special Disney magic.

i   Festival of the Masters — This is an open area celebration of all things artistic. Award-winning artists and musicians are on hand displaying their artwork — and often creating art before your eyes!

ii   Festival of the Seasons — Share the magic of winter decorations, great entertainment, and even a photo opportunity with Santa Claus during this popular evening event.

22 **Free Chocolate!** — Head to Ghirardelli Soda Fountain & Chocolate Shop to get your free chocolate square sample at the door.

23 **Free "Kids Water Park"** — Your kids will love playing around, in and through the interactive fountains, especially during the hot summer months. The fountains are embedded into the ground in cool, soft play areas. You can find these in places like Epcot as well, so remember to always bring swimsuits for the kids — not just to the pool, but to the parks and Downtown Disney as well!

24 **Play with LEGO®** — The LEGO® Imagination Center has a FREE 3,000-square-foot outdoor play area filled with thousands of LEGO blocks, so let your kids play, create, and be inspired by some of the amazing Lego sculptures on display. Kids can also build cars and race with other guests.

i   **Bonus Tip:** Join in the FREE LEGO® Store Monthly Mini Model Build! Your kids (ages 6–14) can learn how to build a cool mini model, and take it home — for free! (One per child, and quantities are limited). There is a new model available every month. Ask a Store Associate for details or visit http://stores.lego.com/en-us/Orlando/events.aspx

25 Free Attractions!

There are countless free "attractions" located throughout Walt Disney World! Here are just a few ways to have fun for free!

i   **Ride the monorail!** Take a ride past (and through!) the Magic Kingdom Resorts or enjoy a trip through Epcot on the Express Monorail from the Transportation and Ticket Center.

> **DID YOU KNOW?** The WDW Monorail System is the most heavily traveled passenger monorail system in the world. It carries an average of 150,000 passengers every day and every year carries more than 50 million people.

ii   **Boat Rides!** Like the monorail, many of the boats in Walt Disney World are more than simply a means of transportation. They're fun and relaxing — and free!

a.   Ride the Friendship boats around Crescent Lake and to World Showcase at Epcot

b.   Take one of the many water taxis to the three monorail resorts and the Magic Kingdom or visit Ft. Wilderness and Wilderness Lodge — get off at any and stop and go exploring (or eating!)

c.   Ride on a pontoon boat down the Sassagoula River from both of the Port Orleans Resorts to and from Downtown Disney

26 **Celebration buttons** — Are you celebrating — a birthday? a honeymoon? anniversary? engagement? a personal milestone? Pick up YOUR free celebration buttons! Stop by the Guest Relations office at any of the theme parks or kiosks and cast members and get your personalized button. This will also help other cast members know you are there for an extra special reason!

27 **Free WiFi!!**

   i   Walt Disney World now offers FREE wireless Internet access in guest rooms and common areas in their resorts. It is also available at the theme parks, Winter Summerland miniature golf course and Disney's Wide World of Sports Complex. You're on vacation, so leave the computer at home... but send and share photos of your family having fun!

   ii   If you want to learn more about how to use technology and social media on your Disney vacation, tune in to WDW Radio Show #283.

28 **Drinks are on Me! (well, Disney)!** — In Epcot, check out Club Cool located near Innoventions West in Future World. Here you can sample — for free — Coca Cola products from around the world. This refreshing area provides 3 ounce sample cups, which enable you to test out (as often as you'd like) eight flavors of Coke products from around the world. It's a refreshment and a social studies lesson all in one!

29 <u>Visit the Tri-Circle-D Ranch</u> — It's free to visit and park at the Tri-Circle-D Ranch (get it? Tri-circle? Like a hidden Mickey?) at Disney's Fort Wilderness Resort & Campground. The ranch is home to the horses that pull the Main Street, U.S.A. trolleys, and also offers a variety of wonderful experiences (both complimentary or at a small cost) for kids and adults.

i   Visit the horse barn and take a look at the magnificent Dragon Calliope, a horse-drawn musical instrument that Walt Disney purchased to be used in the parades at Disneyland in the 1950s, and was also featured in the Disney film, *Toby Tyler*. It was moved to Walt Disney World in 1981 for the Tencennial and was used for numerous parades.

ii   You can also explore the Walt Disney Horses Room, which features photographs of Walt Disney with his beloved horses.

iii   Kids can wander through the blacksmith's shop and visit the petting farm to watch or pet several different animals. It's fun (and educational... just don't tell the kids that they're learning while they're having such a good time!)

   a.   Other Low-Cost Activities:

   • **Horseback Riding** — Enjoy a 45-minute guided-tour through the Sherwood Forest of the Fort Wilderness Resort on an Arabian or quarter horse. Great for new riders, it is for ages 9 and up and is $42 per person. For more information you can call (407) 939-7529.

   • **Pony Rides** — Available for children under 80 pounds and costs around $5 per child. Kids don't want to ride? That's OK. They can pet the ponies for free. No reservations required.

30 **Watch the Electrical Water Pageant** — The Electrical Water Pageant is a floating musical parade that premiered on October 25, 1971 and has been performed nightly on the Seven Seas Lagoon in front of the Magic Kingdom (weather permitting) ever since. It can be viewed from a variety of locations at the Magic Kingdom resorts — for free! And listen carefully, as you'll certainly recognize songs from *The Little Mermaid, Peter Pan, 20,000 Leagues Under the Sea* and other familiar favorites!

i   The Electrical Water Pageant runs about 10 minutes in length and passes in front of the Magic Kingdom and all of the nearby resorts on Bay Lake and the Seven Seas Lagoon. Approximate viewing times:

a.   Disney's Polynesian Resort — 9:00 pm

b.   Disney's Grand Floridian Resort & Spa — 9:15 pm

c.   Disney's Wilderness Lodge — 9:35 pm

d.   Disney's Fort Wilderness Resort & Campground — 9:45 pm/Disney's Contemporary Resort — 10:05 pm

e.   Magic Kingdom park — 10:20 pm *(during extended Magic Kingdom Park hours only)*

ii   **Viewing Tips:** One of my favorite places to watch the Electrical Water Pageant is from the beach or pool area at Disney's Polynesian Resort. Grab a Dole Whip from inside Captain Cook's and enjoy your cool pineapple treat while you watch. Then, stay and watch Wishes Nighttime Spectacular over the Magic Kingdom — the music is piped in to the beach and pool areas. *(Note that nightly fireworks times vary, so check with the resort for the daily schedule)*

> **DID YOU KNOW?** During the summers of 1972 and 1973, The Wonderful World of Water Ski Show ran five times daily on the Seven Seas lagoon. Guests needed a D ticket to watch the shows from a special viewing area. Kite acts, water skiers, and even Goofy and Donald were part of the short-lived production.

31 **Fireworks** — You can enjoy some of Walt Disney World's majestic fireworks shows without having to visit the parks!

    i   Hop on a monorail and watch (and hear!) Wishes Nighttime Spectacular from:

       a.   The beach at Disney's Polynesian Resort

       b.   The bridge at Disney's Contemporary Resort that connects it to Bay Lake Tower

       c.   The boat dock at Disney's Grand Floridian Resort & Spa

    ii   You can see (just the very tops of) Epcot's IllumiNations: Reflections of Earth fireworks show from the beach at Disney's Yacht & Beach Club Resort or the bridge connecting the Boardwalk to the Walt Disney World Swan and Dolphin Resorts. You can also wander to Epcot's "back entrance" at the International Gateway and get an obstructed view from there as well.

32 **Walk (Jog or Bike) Along the Wilderness Trails** — You can explore and enjoy the trails between Disney's Wilderness Lodge and Fort Wilderness Resort and Campground during the daytime to experience Walt Disney World as you never have before.

i   You can follow the 2.5 mile "Exercise Trail" (although you can simply stroll through it) and see everything from local (no so-wild) wildlife to untouched natural landscapes. The trail is both paved and sand-covered.

ii   There is also a ¾ mile "Swamp Trail" that follows the shores of Bay Lake as well.
Take a walk, jog (or rent a bicycle!) and head out for a quiet morning along the trails!

33 **Winter Holiday Decorations** — Mid-November through early January can truly be regarded as the most wonderful time of the year at Walt Disney World, as you can experience the holiday spirit and magic every day — for free. Beyond the special events like Mickey's Very Merry Christmas Party in the Magic Kingdom, the Epcot Holiday Storyteller Around the World and the Osborne Family Spectacle of Dancing Lights at Disney's Hollywood Studios, there are so many wonderful ways to celebrate the season at Walt Disney World — for free!

i   **At the Resorts** — Visit any (or ALL!) of the Disney resorts during the holidays. Because the theming throughout the parks and resorts varies greatly, the types of decorations and stories to be told in the resorts differ as well. From period ornamentation at Disney's Boardwalk resort to a 70-foot tall Gingerbread Holiday Tree featuring nearly 35,800 white LED lights at Disney's Contemporary Resort to a life-sized (and yes, edible) gingerbread house at the Grand Floridian, there is something unique to enjoy in each of the hotel's lobbies.

a.   **Bonus Tip**: On Christmas Eve and Christmas Day, you can usually meet some Christmas/Santa-themed characters in the lobby of the resort hotels, along with carolers

ii   **In The Parks** — While you will need admission to the Disney Parks, most of the holiday festivities are included at no extra cost. From snowfall on Main Street USA and shimmering lights on Cinderella Castle in the Magic Kingdom, to Holiday Storytellers around the World in Epcot, the Osborne Family Spectacle of Dancing Lights (over 6 million of them!) at Disney's Hollywood Studios and the Jingle Jungle Parade in Disney's Animal Kingdom, each park celebrates the season in their own, wonderful ways! Visit the Walt Disney World Holidays web page for more information: http://disneyworld.disney.go.com/holidays

34   **Create an International Souvenir!** When visiting Epcot, you can stop by each of the nations in World Showcase and allow your children to visit Kidcot Stations. At these stations, children will be presented with a Duffy the Bear craft that they can carry to each World Showcase nation. When visiting, students can add international touches and interact with cast members from the host nation.

35   **Transportation Cards** — When you are using the complimentary transportation, ask your monorail, bus, or boat drivers if they have transportation trading cards. Not all drivers will, but don't give up! The cards make a great souvenir, and the hunt for them can become a fun family adventure!

36   **Business Cards** — On Main Street, USA in the Magic Kingdom and on Sunset Boulevard in Disney's Hollywood Studios, ask the "streetmosphere" characters if they have a business card. Some do, and they make for a fun souvenir for your scrapbook. Make sure you take your picture with these characters too, so you have a visual record of who they were when you are back home reflecting on the day.

37 **Stickers Galore!** If you enjoy making scrapbooks.... You will find many opportunities to collect stickers to embellish your memory pages! Outside many shops, by the turnstiles, and often by DVC kiosks, cast members will distribute an assortment of Disney character stickers to children and parents alike! While many people like to put them on their shirts and hats, you can also keep some and use them later to add an extra magical Disney touch to those autograph books and photo albums.

38 **Free Training** — Did you know you can learn a new occupation while you are on vacation? Well, that is, if you want to become a pirate or a Jedi in your next career! Family-friendly "training" is available:

i **Yo Ho Yo Ho, A Pirate's Life for Me!** Attend the Pirate Tutorial in Adventureland in the Magic Kingdom and learn from Captain Jack himself (and his pirate friends) the fine art of piracy on the high seas! Check your Magic Kingdom times guide to find out when these sessions will be held!

ii **Use the Force!** The Jedi Training Academy at Disney Hollywood Studios near Star Tours also offers free training to young Star Wars fans. Be sure to check your times guide for information about pre-registering for this interactive activity featuring some of our favorite Star Wars villains.

   a. Check out this video about the Jedi Training Academy!

   b. Participants who are selected will receive a commemorative certificate.

iii Become a detective in Agent P's World Showcase Adventure. Included with the price of admission, this quest allows you to work with the beloved Phineas & Ferb to solve mysteries throughout the nations of the World Showcase.

39   **Become an Artist!** While we are looking into learning new skills, why not try your hand at becoming an animator? In the post-show area of the Art of Animation, join in the Animation Academy, where a Disney animator will teach you how to draw a Disney character, and you can keep your art!

40   **Book a Magic Your Way Package** and receive freebies and vouchers, including

    i   Free luggage tags

    ii   Free voucher for one round of miniature golf

    iii   100 free game points for resort arcades

    iv   Vouchers for discounts at Planet Hollywood, Spa Services, Bass Fishing, and the Children's Activity Centers.

RESOURCES AND LINKS

http://WDWRadio.com — Your Walt Disney World Information Station. Home of Lou Mongello's award-winning podcast, blog, videos, live broadcasts, special events, discussion forums and much more!

Lou Mongello's Walt Disney World Trivia Books, Audio Tours of Walt Disney World and official WDW Radio Logo Gear — http://WDWRadio.com/Shop

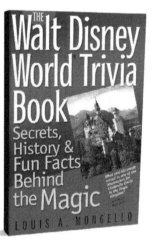

Learn more about Lou Mongello and book him to speak at
http://LouMongello.com

Lou's Picks — Some of Lou's favorite Disney books, movies, music and more. http://WDWRadio.com/Resources

Download the **FREE WDW Radio app** for your iPhone, iPad, Android or Kindle device — http://WDWRadio.com/app

Connect with Lou Mongello and WDW Radio

Twitter — @LouMongello

Facebook — http://Facebook.com/LouMongello

Facebook (WDW Radio page) — http://Facebook.com/WDWRadio

Pinterest — http://pinterest.com/LouMongello

Instagram — http://instagram.com/LouMongello

YouTube — http://YouTube.com/WDWRadio

Ustream.tv — http://ustream.tv/wdwradio

Mouse Fan Travel — My recommended travel provider — http://MouseFanTravel.com

The official Walt Disney World Resort © web site — http://DisneyWorld.com

Photos courtesy of Cory Disbrow—
Visit his Disney Photography Blog
and Disney Photography eBooks and apps
at DisneyPhotographyBlog.com

102
WAYS
TO SAVE MONEY
FOR AND AT
WALT DISNEY WORLD
BY LOU MONGELLO